The impact of economic democracy
Profit-sharing and employee-shareholding schemes

Do profit sharing and employee shareholding help to reduce inflation and unemployment? What impact do such schemes have on productivity and employee satisfaction? Do they improve industrial relations?

These fundamental questions are explored in this unique study of profit-sharing and employee-shareholding schemes. A companion volume to *The Origins of Economic Democracy*, which focused on the origins of profit-sharing schemes, this book concentrates on their impact on the economic, industrial relations, and organizational performance of companies.

The authors analyse international research findings and research data from over 1,000 British companies and report on interviews with nearly 2,000 employees to demonstrate that there is indeed a link between the economic performance of companies and profit sharing. However, the relationship is a complex one: industrial relations may be improved by schemes, but good employers are likely to introduce profit sharing in any case; and though attitudes to work do change, schemes have more immediate impact on satisfaction and communications than on productivity and effort put into work.

These conclusions will be of great interest to academics and business people alike, lending support to the case for expanding economic democracy and casting new light on an issue of international importance.

The Authors

Michael Poole is Professor of Human Resource Management at Cardiff Business School, University of Wales, College of Cardiff. Glenville Jenkins is Senior Lecturer in Management at the West Glamorgan Institute of Higher Education, Swansea.

The impact of economic democracy

Profit-sharing and employee-shareholding schemes

Michael Poole
and
Glenville Jenkins

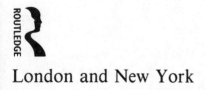

London and New York

First published 1990
by Routledge
11 New Fetter Lane, London EC4P 4EE

Simultaneously published in the USA and Canada
by Routledge
a division of Routledge, Chapman and Hall, Inc.
29 West 35th Street, New York, NY 10001

Typeset by Pat and Anne Murphy, Highcliffe-on-Sea, Dorset

Printed in Great Britain by Billing & Sons Ltd, Worcester

British Library Cataloguing in Publication Data

Poole, Michael, *1943–*
   The Impact of Economic Democracy: Profit-sharing and
   employee-shareholding schemes.
   1. Great Britain, companies, employees, personnel
   I. Title   II. Jenkins, Glenville, *1951–*
   331.21640941

   ISBN 0-415-03587-2

Library of Congress Cataloging in Publication Data

Jenkins, Glenville, 1951–
   The Impact of Economic Democracy: Profit-sharing and employee-
shareholding schemes / Glenville Jenkins and Michael Poole.
      p.   cm.
   Includes bibliographical references (p.
   ISBN 0-415-03587-2
   1. Profit-sharing – Great Britain.   2. Employee stock options –
Great Britain.   3. Industrial relations – Great Britain.
4. Job satisfaction – Great Britain.   5. Organizational
change – Great Britain.   I. Poole, Michael.   II. Title.
   HD302.5.A4J46   1990   89-70215
   331.2'164–dc20   CIP

Contents

Figure

Tables

Tables

Tables

Preface

This is the second volume of a study concerning profit-sharing and employee-shareholding schemes in the company. The first book involved an account of the origins and development of schemes, while the second entails an assessment of their consequences for the economic and industrial relations peformance of companies, the degree of satisfaction of employees, and the extent to which the introduction of profit-sharing and other related practices has occasioned changes in work practices and organizational flexibility.

The data presented in the two monographs derive from a project initiated in the Social Science Branch of the Department of Employment and sponsored by this particular governmental department. The early design work was undertaken by Gillian Smith who subsequently produced an article from the survey stage of the research entitled 'Profit sharing and employee share ownership in Britain' for the *Employment Gazette* (September 1986, pp 380–5). There were two principal phases to the project: (1) a survey of companies in Britain; and (2) case studies of selected firms derived from the enterprises included in Stage 1.

The survey commenced with a series of short telephone screening interviews in 1,125 companies that were designed to obtain information on the extent of profit-sharing and employee-shareholding schemes in Britain and to provide a sample for subsequent detailed interviews. This was followed by the so-called 'main stage' survey of 303 firms in Britain in which a wide range of data was gathered on the operation of schemes and the factors associated with their adoption or non-adoption. The questionnaires for the survey were developed jointly by IFF Research Limited, DE Social Science Branch, and Michael Poole. The fieldwork was carried out in May 1985 by IFF under the direction of Judy Morrell. In August 1985, a data tape was transferred to the University of Wales College of Cardiff (UWCC) to enable Michael Poole to conduct a more detailed analysis of the survey material. At this point, Joan Wright carried out the necessary computing work with considerable speed and skill.

At the design stage of the research, it was recognized that a further case study phase would be necessary in order to allow for a detailed exploration of the specific processes which lead companies to introduce profit sharing and the problems encountered developing schemes. Above all, it was considered important that an assessment should be made of the views of employees. In consequence, the Department of Employment commissioned Michael Poole to carry out the case study phase which included: (1) detailed interviews with key management respondents; (2) interviews with full-time trade union officers and lay representatives; (3) the gathering of data on company performance; and (4) the administering of a questionnaire to a substantial number of employees (approximately 2,000).

The case study phase of the research commenced in spring 1986 and involved 22 companies selected from the 303 firms in the 'main stage' survey. To ensure a regional balance, the companies were divided equally between South Wales/the South West of England and London/the South East of England (further details and the methods used appear in the Appendices). The case study phase was directed by Michael Poole, while Glenville Jenkins and Michael Gasiorek provided research assistance.

During the survey stage of the research Francis Butler was integrally involved in the project and Peter Brannen chaired various meetings of both the survey and case study phases. Towards the end of the case studies, Neil Millward assumed chairmanship of the steering committee meetings. At UWCC, Brian Moores and Andy Thompson provided valuable advice on statistical techniques for handling the survey data.

Throughout the survey and case study stages, Gillian Smith handled the project with considerable skill and thoroughness. Valuable comments were provided by members of the steering committee for the case studies and especially by Stephen Creigh, John Cullinane, Dorothy Green and Michael Lott. In the case study companies, there were many respondents who gave considerably of their knowledge and time and, without such assistance, the project could not have been a success. The comments of Euan Cameron were particularly insightful in this respect. Richard Long helped considerably by providing a copy of a questionnaire from his own research which helped to inform many of the items in the employee attitudes survey. IFF Research and, especially, Judy Morrell, offered very valuable assistance to the UWCC research team to secure contacts with the case study companies. Moreover, for their considerable efforts in typing this monograph a special word of thanks is due to Marina Miller and Karen Owen.

It is hoped that the two volumes of this study on profit-sharing and employee-shareholding schemes, *The Origins of Economic Democracy* (published in 1989) and the current volume will help to shed considerable light on the operation of profit-sharing and share-ownership schemes in Britain. The Department of Employment deserves particular gratitude for funding the research though, naturally, any views expressed are those of the authors and do not necessarily reflect those of the funding body.

Michael Poole and Glenville Jenkins

Chapter one

Introduction

Profit-sharing and employee-shareholding schemes may be interpreted from a number of distinctive vantage points. In the first place, they may be understood in terms of the spread of ownership rights to the workforce. On this view, the aim is to eradicate permanently the longstanding antagonism and opposition of capital and labour. Secondly, they may be linked with policies on employee participation and organizational democracy, with the objective of increasing the sense of identity of employees with the companies in which they work. And thirdly, the case may be advanced in terms of competitiveness. Profit sharing and employee shareholding are seen to advance this through improved motivation and commitment of the workforce, together with greater flexibility and adaptability and higher levels of productivity and profitability. Moreover, these policies are further linked with the broader economic objectives of reducing unemployment and inflation.

These various arguments in favour of employee financial participation are examined in depth and detail in this volume. But it is essential to point out at the outset that there are many and varied forms of this phenomenon, the effects of which will probably not be homogeneous. For example, ownership rights are likely to be enhanced most dramatically through producer cooperatives and worker buyouts. By contrast, profit sharing through share schemes may be sufficient to occasion a sense of participation. And cash-based forms of profit sharing are likely to have the most immediate and direct effects so far as competitiveness is concerned.

Financial participation by employees is thus a complex and multi-dimensional phenomenon. The first volume on this issue, *The Origins of Economic Democracy*, was designed to uncover the forces which underpin the growth of profit-sharing and share-ownership schemes and their varied rates of adoption by companies. This second volume has a different focus: to examine the consequences of the introduction of schemes for company and

1

individual performance. In the first chapter, the growing literature on this issue is examined in relation to the economic, industrial relations and organizational impact of schemes. This is followed by the specification of a number of analytical frameworks and models in Chapter 2. Evidence from the Department of Employment sponsored research of profit sharing and share ownership is then examined in relation to the impact of schemes. Following this analysis, the varied sets of data are interlinked by means of detailed case studies. Finally, an evaluation of the consequences of profit-sharing and employee-shareholding schemes is undertaken in relation to the main debates on this subject in Britain and overseas.

Profit-sharing and share-ownership schemes are connected with a number of diverse forms of industrial organization where at least part of the equity is owned by the workforce and/or part of total employee remuneration is linked with the profit performance as an addition to existing pay arrangements. In the first volume of this study we showed that the number of profit-sharing and share-ownership schemes in the late 1970s and 1980s has expanded considerably, even though only a minority of employees is currently covered by schemes of this type. It was also observed that growth has particularly occurred in firms in the financial sector and in companies with managements broadly committed to developing employee involvement. Moreover, there is no doubt that the recent advancement of schemes has been stimulated by facilitative legislation and tax incentives. And the expansion of schemes can also be linked with the wider share ownership movement as a whole (Grout, 1987).

Turning, then, in this volume to examine the impact of schemes, profit-sharing and share-ownership schemes are widely held to have had a substantial potential effect upon economic and industrial organization. This potential is embodied in a complex of economic, industrial relations, sociological and psychological interpretations. For economists, profit sharing is viewed as a way to improve a company's financial performance and to control inflation, increase levels of employment, improve the distribution of wealth and occasion economic stability. For the industrial relations scholar, it is seen as radically influencing the relationship between managers, employees and unions, redesigning methods of remuneration and reducing conflict and antagonism in the workplace. For the sociologist, the impact is in terms of changing the nature of social relations and attitudes to work. And, for the psychologist, improvements in morale and motivation of the workforce are envisaged resulting in higher output and productivity in the firm as a whole. The breadth of the potential impact thus makes an understanding of the more substantive consequences of profit-sharing and share-ownership schemes a vital consideration.

For us there are three issues which are central to the debates on the potential effects of profit-sharing and share-ownership schemes. These are: (1) the economic impact of profit sharing; (2) the impact on industrial relations; and (3) the effects on organizational performance expressed in terms of employee efforts to work harder, to eliminate waste, to improve efficiency, to increase quality and to reduce costs.

Economic impact of profit sharing

The economic assessment of the consequences of profit-sharing and share-ownership schemes has been developed at both macro and micro levels. The first refers to the wider economy and the second to the firm or company level.

Macro-economic impact

To begin with, then, economists have been concerned with the impact of profit-sharing arrangements on the macro-economic performance of nations and have stressed that workers are being priced out of jobs because the present wages system is inflexible and inefficient. On this view, profit-sharing and share-ownership schemes occasion a reduction in unemployment and in inflation by making wages more responsive to changes in economic performance. This occurs by means of the 'sliding scale' principle which links a proportion of wages to profits and/or sales of the company. As sales or profits decline so does profit related pay. Moreover, it is further argued that if labour costs are proportional to total costs, labour costs will have less of an impact on prices and create greater employment flexibility. As a consequence, employers will be unlikely to make workers redundant. Hence, a radical and universal reform of the remuneration system, where a proportion of wages is linked to profits or sales, would reduce both unemployment and inflation.

Undoubtedly the most influential assessment of the macro-economic impact of profit sharing is contained in Weitzman's *The Share Economy* (1984). However, Weitzman is best envisaged as part of a long tradition of economists who have advocated the introduction of some form of profit-sharing scheme, his predecessors including Keynes (1940), Meade (1964) and Kelso and Adler (1958). Central to Weitzman's argument is that lack of wage flexibility is one of the basic causes of both unemployment and

3

inflation. He thus proposes the transition from existing economic relations to a share economy where the labour market would experience a constant excess demand for labour and in which permanent full employment at competitive remuneration, no inflation and an improvement in working conditions and employee attitudes have been effected.

Weitzman's solution to wage inflexibility and thereby unemployment and inflation is thus to create a new universal remuneration system in which profit sharing plays an important role. This new system is made up of two components: (a) a base wage as under existing payment systems; and (b) a profit related wage – a proportion of the per capita profit earned by the company. Under this payment system, an employer will hire more workers if the added fixed cost of each additional worker is less than the added revenue that this worker will produce. Although the hiring of more workers will reduce profit per worker (and hence their level of remuneration), total profits will increase.

However, there are many criticisms of Weitzman's macro-economic analysis, and these centre on the problems of implementation and the extent of the schemes impact on existing economic relations. These are examined in terms of: (a) employee risk; (b) the arbitrary nature of profit sharing; and (c) the employment and inflationary impact.

In contrast to Weitzman's view, *wage inflexibility* may be explained in terms of *wage stability* which highlights the risk-adversity strategies of employees. In particular, contracts are entered into with the employer precisely to avoid the wage flexibility that can have a substantial impact on the employee's own financial planning in the domestic sphere. Profit-sharing schemes can thus expose workers to a significant and unacceptable amount of income risk. And even if profit sharing is share based, the risk may be all the more substantial since a declining share price can lead to a dwindling rather than appreciating asset for the workers concerned. Moreover, profit-sharing schemes are potentially arbitrary and unfair in that the locus of decision-making over the distribution of income/profits lies outside employee influence and may bear only an indirect relationship with a particular worker's efforts.

Nevertheless, recent American research gives some indirect support to Weitzman's arguments concerning *employment* and suggests that employment growth is particularly likely in firms where employees have share option schemes and therefore own a proportion of the equity. Thus Rosen and Klein (1983) examined employment growth in 43 employee owned companies (including cooperatives) and found that employment in these companies grew nearly three times as fast as in traditional firms.

However, it should be noted that growth in employment could occasion further problems. Current workers and their union representatives may wish to prevent the firm from hiring extra individuals because any expansion in employment drives down the existing employees' remuneration (Blanchflower and Oswald, 1987; Mitchell, 1987). And large variations in pay between firms may conflict with the principle of equal pay for equal work (Derrick, 1969: 158; Mitchell, 1987). Employers may actually prefer more wage stability than employment stability for, under conditions of full employment, employees will, in the short run, quickly move to firms offering higher total wages. Furthermore, the increased level of employee turnover could be detrimental to economic efficiency in the short term. It is likely, therefore, that employers and workers may have considerable opposition to such a fundamental change in their remuneration systems. Indeed, wage pressures on the share economy are likely to be considerable.

Moreover, so far as inflation is concerned, the share economy may be inherently unstable. Indeed it may be inflationary if a wage component is maintained and the profit component of pay comprises an additional element in the total remuneration package of employees (see Mitchell, 1987; Blanchflower and Oswald, 1987).

In principle, of course, opposition to change in the remunerâtion systems can be overcome by: (1) tax incentives in the short run; and (2) reduced employee involvement in the long run (Weitzman, 1985a). But against this, such subsidies may turn out to be merely cosmetic with both management and unions colluding over pay and profit levels (see Burton, 1986; Blanchflower and Oswald, 1987). Secondly, an essential political component in the share economy is that employee involvement in decision-making (and particularly on employment decisions) should be minimized. Above all, a reduction in the influence of trade union and collective bargaining machinery and other forms of employee organization which may affect the labour market is viewed as essential. Hence, the reduction of employee participation, a cornerstone of Weitzman's argument, is a development which would run counter to ongoing trends in this direction and to the tendency for various types of employee involvement to be interconnected (see Volume 1).

Micro-economic impact

Economists have also been concerned with the micro-economic effects of profit sharing and particularly with the consequences for company performance. Briefly, both company profitability and worker productivity are seen as likely to improve following the introduction of profit-sharing schemes. Given such major claims for the impact of profit-sharing schemes, it is thus important to examine in more detail the micro-economic consequences of profit sharing.

A wide range of studies (and notably from the USA) have pointed to a relationship between profit-sharing and share-ownership schemes and company economic and financial performance. Generally, firms which have profit-sharing arrangements have been shown to outperform non-profit-sharing firms. This applies to profits as a percentage of net worth and income, turnover, net worth, dividends and share price (Metger and Colletti, 1971; Conte and Tannenbaum, 1978). In the UK, too, in an analysis of share valuations in the retail sector, Richardson and Nejad (1986) have argued that financial participation occasions a significant improvement in company performance on the stock market. Moreover, they provide some support for the proposition that a strong managerial commitment to profit-sharing and share-ownership schemes improves performance as well. Furthermore, as was shown in Volume 1 of our study, there is a clear link between the adoption of schemes, and trends in business volume and annual turnover of companies.

Yet, despite these and other research findings which we will examine shortly, there still remains some doubt as to whether companies perform better because they have profit-sharing and share-ownership schemes; or whether they are successful companies which would perform well even without such schemes but feel they should share the success of the company with their employees.

Profitability

To analyse these arguments further, the effects of employee financial participation on profitability and productivity are examined in greater depth. Although British research on the impact of profit-sharing and share-ownership schemes on the economic performance of companies is relatively limited, in the USA several studies have examined this relationship. In one of the earliest of these, Conte and Tannenbaum (1978) compared the profitability of 30 companies with employee ownership arrangements. They found that those companies with employee ownership arrangements were 1.5 times more profitable than those firms of comparable size which did not have such arrangements. More recently, Wagner (1984) found that companies with at least ten per cent employee share ownership performed equally as well on overall returns on investment as other companies in the same industry. Moreover, on net operating margin, growth of sales, book value/share and return on equity, firms with employee ownership outperformed the other companies studied by 62–75 per cent.

However, the research findings are not entirely consistent. Indeed, Livingstone and Henry (1980), Bhagat, Brickley and Lease (1984) and Edwards (1987) discovered that, on average, employee share ownership had an adverse affect on profitability. Moreover, Brooks, Henry and Livingstone (1982) found that employee share-ownership schemes (ESOPs) had no significant effect on profits. Similarly, in a survey of 100 companies with employee-ownership schemes, Tannenbaum, Cooke and Lohmann (1984) found that profitability and financial growth did not differ significantly from firms without employee ownership schemes. Companies with schemes, however, were found to have a higher rate of survival during the period of the study (1976 to 1982).

None the less, it should be stressed that some inconsistency in the findings is not surprising, since employees' efforts in improving the profits of their firm may be counterbalanced by events outside their control. Indeed, the impact of external events on company profitability may enhance or reduce profits within a typical firm regardless of the initiatives or efforts of the majority of employees.

Productivity

The impact on productivity is primarily concerned with *incentives* and, according to Nuti (1987: 24), the viability of profit sharing 'depends in large measure on these productivity-enhancing effects'. It is hypothesized that the introduction of profit-sharing schemes will create an incentive to work harder and more effectively in order to improve profits. Unlike traditional incentives which link individual effort to reward, profit-sharing schemes are a social or group incentive where the efforts of all employees contribute to improved rewards (either through cash or shares). This form of group incentive is organizationally based and, because it leaves considerable discretion to employees to avoid increasing their productive effort, it may increase the need for management supervision as well. None the less, such disadvantages can be avoided if the incentive is linked to work or peer groups at the level of the task, with employees acting as monitors of other workers' performance. As Nuti (1987: 23–4) as proposed:

A productivity increase can be expected (at no cost to the workers) as a result of intelligent and effective use of any given individual level of effort, cooperating with other workers and management, and monitoring and supervising each other's effort, efficiency and cooperation.

Indeed, the impact on productivity may be particularly strong where there is: (a) a limited number of employees; and (b) individual employees can link their increased effort or productivity directly to profits performance.

There is also some, albeit limited, empirical evidence to support the view that increased employee commitment in the profit-sharing firm raises productivity levels. This conclusion is suggested by American studies which have compared commitment and productivity in employee-owned plywood firms and supermarkets with traditional firms in the same industries (Bellas, 1972; Greenberg, 1984). Furthermore, Marsh and McAllister (1981) examined 128 US companies with Employee Stock Ownership Plan (ESOP) schemes and found that, on average, *productivity* increased 0.78 per cent per annum in these firms compared with an average decrease of 0.74 per cent for a weighted national sample of similar companies.

Impact on industrial relations

The case for extending employee financial participation has also been articulated in terms of the impact on industrial relations. There are a number of partly separate and partly interlinked arguments here which relate to: (a) management–union relations generally; (b) industrial conflict (including strikes and rates of absenteeism and labour turnover); (c) managerial authority relations; and (d) trade unions and collective bargaining.

Management–union relations

The change in employee status from employee to employee shareholder may thus have implications for industrial relations within the company. In principle, employee shareholders may be considered to be a fairly homogenous and identifiable group with common interests both in terms of their corporate investment and in their employment relationship with the company and, as such, their collective interests may differ from those of the ordinary employee. This has implications for existing channels of representation and participation, particularly through trade unions.

Above all, it is conceivable that, as a result of increasing their identification with other shareholders and with the company, employee shareholders may perceive little need for collective representation of their interests by trade unions. This may mean that the position of trade unions in the company could be weakened and a schism created between ordinary employees and employee shareholders, thereby reducing the level of solidarity in the union (Webb and Webb, 1914). Alternatively, if employee shareholders retain an instrumental orientation to work, their attitudes may not differ markedly from those of ordinary employees and the importance of the wage/effort bargain may still be dominant. On this view, the trade union traditional role will be little changed. However, employee shareholders, because of their common interest with other employees and improved status as shareholders, may seek additional individual or collective participation in decision-making through the union. And, if the majority of employees are shareholders, this could significantly change the traditional adversarial or conflictual role of trade unions to one of providing an alternative to managerial expertise in the efficient running of the company. Conversely, it could extend the range of conflict to encompass areas where management is viewed as not performing its traditional functions.

Industrial conflict

Turning more specifically to industrial conflict, it has long been argued that one of the main effects of profit-sharing schemes is the reduction of conflict in the workplace (Webb and Webb, 1914). Some recent research has also pointed to this conclusion (Long, 1978a; Estrin and Wilson, 1986). However, there still remains some ambiguity as to the impact of ownership on industrial conflict. While Long (1978a) and Estrin and Wilson (1986) have suggested that employee ownership reduces conflict; others, such as Meade (1986), have argued that profit sharing could increase it. By contrast, Stern *et al* (1983) have proposed that industrial conflict will decrease in the short term because of the employees' efforts either to protect jobs or to increase profits or both; but increase in the long term and become more intense because of dissatisfaction with the control structures in the enterprise that typically obtain under most profit-sharing and share-ownership arrangements.

But industrial conflict itself is a multidimensional phenomenon with both attitudinal and behavioural dimensions. It may well be, therefore, that any assessment of the impact of profit sharing and employee share ownership requires a detailed analysis of various aspects of conflict such as strikes, labour turnover and absenteeism (see, for example, Estrin and Wilson, 1986). Indeed, it may be the case that there are variable consequences of the introduction of schemes on each of these (and on other) dimensions of conflict itself.

Managerial authority relations

Employee share ownership is also thought to have implications for managerial authority relations. Indeed, on one view, the employee is placed in a position to delegate the running of the company to management. However, in reality, the increasing diversification of share ownership effectively means that the status of the employee shareholder is little different from that of the small investor, whose impact on company affairs is undoubtedly marginal. Therefore, little real influence in the day-to-day running of the company can be expected from minority shareholders such as those in share-ownership schemes.

Indeed, although employee financial participation and decision-making involvement are linked, share-ownership schemes are rarely accompanied by significant relocation of control as in the case of cooperatives or totally owned employee concerns (Woodworth, 1981b; Russell, 1984). In certain cases, as in the majority of recent privatized companies in the UK, workers have received a substantial number of shares as a gift (or fringe benefit) but without gaining significant ground in exercising greater influence or participation in decision-making. Furthermore, there is said to be little expectation of control under these arrangements (Hammer and Stern, 1980; Long, 1981, 1982).

The legitimate basis for managerial authority to control the enterprise rests not only upon expertise in running the company but also on property rights. Employee share ownership potentially affects the property relation of managerial authority when employees purchase shares in the firm. As shareholders, employees attain additional financial interests in their companies. However, as with other shareholders, the employee shareholder delegates operational responsibility to management for the efficient performance of the company and a sufficient return on his or her investment. Employee shareholders have no joint ownership over the property or assets of the company or little direct influence over its personnel. Their rights remain limited to those of liability and interest on shares they own. Thus, particularly in large organizations, mere share ownership often amounts to a situation of little real influence by minority shareholders.

Share ownership does, however, confer certain rights on the shareholder such as electing the board of directors, the right to financial information about the company and participation in the annual general meeting. Moreover, Long (1981: 49) has argued that employee shareholders are in a stronger position than the typical shareholder in a large company. This is because employee share-holders have access to much more information and knowledge about the company simply because they work there. Employee shareholders are concentrated within the organization and not dispersed as is the case with other shareholders. Employee share-holders in the company are, therefore, a fairly homogenous and readily identifiable group with common interests based on a specific employment relationship. It is possible, therefore, that the collective representation of employee shareholders interests may, as we shall see, effectively counter managerial expertise on certain issues either through shareholder institutions (the company board) or through traditional avenues of employee representation (collective bargaining).

Trade unions and collective bargaining

But, so far as industrial relations are concerned, no issue is more fundamental than the potential impact of employee financial parti-cipation on trade unions. As has been noted earlier, profit-sharing and share-ownership schemes can effect a change in the character of the union's constituency from one of representing employees to one of protecting the rights of employee shareholders (Sockell, 1983). But this change is contradictory to the development of traditional trade unionism, being fundamentally opposed to the principles of collective bargaining and trade unionism (see Webb and Webb, 1897, 1914; Cole, 1957). To the extent that profit-sharing schemes reduce labour turnover and labour mobility, they remove a necessary condition for the individual employee to make the best possible bargain with his or her employer. And, as we noted in Volume 1, such schemes may destroy 'the community of interests' on which collective bargaining depends by creating a vertical schism between employees. Hence, they may reduce trade union solidarity and bargaining power.

More recent evaluations of this pessimistic role for trade unions is provided by Hanson (1965), Bradley and Gelb (1983b) and Bradley (1986). Bradley and Gelb (1983b: 57) thus note in their review that the:

. . . transitions to employee ownership appear to be able potentially to weaken the nationwide, traditional role of trade unionism as representative of the working class through the mechanism of collective bargaining.

Bradley (1986: 60−1) has also suggested that profit-sharing arrangements form part of a general demise of union influence through traditional channels, in that:

With limited resources and tight monetary policy, traditional collective bargaining is seen as a zero sum (or negative sum) game, where one man's wage hike is another's unemployment. Thus, a new cooperativism between trade unions and management is encouraged and the focus of industrial relations is shifted away from traditional collective bargaining.

None the less, there is evidence, notably from the American context, to suggest that employee share ownership has not led to a reduced perception for the need for trade unions (see Stern and Hammer, 1978; Long, 1979). This is particularly evident where power relationships continue to remain unequal, as characterized by unequal equity holdings among differing employee groups and a lack of democratic control within the firm. Indeed, in these instances, the perceived necessity for trade unionism may increase in the long term (Long, 1979).

But some changes in the union role under profit-sharing and employee ownership arrangements can be expected (Whyte, 1978 and Jenkins, 1979 quoted in Sockell, 1983; Long, 1980a; Bradley, 1986b; Mitchell, 1987). More specifically, it may be anticipated that the union's role will significantly change if a substantial proportion of wages is linked with profits performance. Paradoxically, however, this may not necessarily be to the detriment of the union. Indeed, shop stewards may increasingly have to deal with the problem of so-called 'accounting manipulation' (*eg* transfer pricing) in order to ensure that the relative share of profits accruing to the membership is reasonable (see also Webb and Webb, 1914). This would require even greater disclosure of information to unions or employee representatives than at present. Moreover, this level of provision would eventually give rise to increased managerial accountability and trade union assessment of management decision-making. As a consequence, the union's normal 'reactive' role (Crouch, 1982) in formal negotiation may change. Above all, a greater role in certain types of decision-making would be required to augment the size of the employees' share of the profits. And the increased expertise needed, particularly with regard to profit allocation, could require a more centralized union structure and possibly a move away from plant level bargaining arrangements.

Indeed, on another set of assumptions, profit sharing may increase unionization. Thus, Mitchell has argued that a profit-sharing system puts non-union employees at a disadvantage in that they have no voice in management decisions which affect their share of the profits. He agrees with the Webbs (1914) that employees could not adequately verify the size of the financial share without the union's organizational expertise and bargaining power. Hence the union's claim to expertise could be crucial to increasing its decision-making and regulatory role and thus its ability to recruit membership amongst profit-sharing participants. But of course such a change would require a modification in traditional union policies towards profit-sharing and share-ownership schemes.

Organizational impact

Nevertheless, there is evidence to suggest that attitudes rather than behaviour are more affected by the introduction of profit-sharing and share-ownership schemes. Bell and Hanson (1984, 1987) have thus reported high levels of support by employees for profit sharing in principle and for company schemes and an increased interest in the profits and financial results of the company. Nearly a half of the respondents (47 per cent) said their loyalty to the firm had been strengthened and just over a half (51 per cent) felt that the schemes made people work more effectively (Bell and Hanson, 1984, 1987; see also Fogarty and White, 1988).

Turning to the third broad area where the impact of profit-sharing and employee-shareholding schemes has been examined, there are several issues of relevance to the potential consequences for organizations. These include: (1) employee involvement; (2) organizational identity; (3) employee satisfaction and commitment; and (4) attitudes to the employment relationship.

Employee involvement

As we have seen in Volume 1, profit-sharing and share-ownership schemes may be initiated by management for a number of reasons among which are to improve the productivity of their employees, increase their sense of loyalty to the company or to augment the level of employees' direct participation in the company. As such they form part of a managerial strategy to influence the level of output, the degree of commitment and the level of joint decision-making between management and employees. Furthermore, it is thought that profit-sharing and particularly share-ownership schemes offer employees the opportunity to increase their involvement in the workplace, improve their level of financial understanding and the degree of communication between employees and management.

Employee participation in ownership has thus been viewed as a means for employees to influence company policy and to share in the rewards of work. For Tannenbaum (1983) and Long (1978a) in particular, employee ownership results in an increase in levels of worker participation and control. After all, through share ownership, employees achieve certain control rights which they would otherwise not possess. Long (1979), for example, has concluded that employee share ownership increases worker influence at organizational policy levels. The employee's desire for worker participation is increased by share ownership because ownership confers a legitimate right to participate in decision-making. It also increases 'organizational identification' which, in turn, leads workers to become more interested in the affairs of their places of work (Long, 1981: 851). These additional rights and stronger organizational identity thus increase the desire of workers for more influence in decision-making at policy, departmental and job levels in the company.

Studies of worker cooperatives have also pointed to improvements in participative arrangements (see Russell, Hochner and Perry, 1979; Greenberg, 1980; Rhodes and Steers, 1981). And other investigations (Long, 1980b; Conte, Tannenbaum and McCullough, 1980; Tannenbaum, Cooke and Lohmann, 1984) have reported that the percentage of company shares owned by employees is positively related to increased employee participation. By contrast some analyses of individual firms (see *eg* Hammer and Stern, 1980) have found no significant relationship between employee ownership and perceived or desired worker influence. Indeed, for Hammer and Stern (1980), share ownership may be associated with a decline in the desire for worker influence (see also French and Rosenstein, 1984).

Hence the research findings on employee participation remain contradictory and do not clearly point to a conclusive relationship between ownership and employee participation in decision-making. However, such research clearly provides some, if limited, evidence of an association between ownership and participation (Klein and Rosen, 1986).

Profit-sharing and share-ownership schemes, then, may impact upon managerial practice and control in organizations by increasing the degree of participation both directly (voting for the board of directors) and indirectly (increasing the level and degree of communications and managements' formal or informal responsiveness to employees' collective interests) (Mitchell, 1987). This may be further enhanced because, as Long (1981) notes, managerial attitudes towards worker participation may be influenced by employee share ownership. First, management may respond to the changed basis of their authority and the increased desire for participation in decision-making brought about by workers' legitimate property rights and increased organizational identity. Secondly, employee share ownership may increase managerial perceptions of the legitimacy of increased employee involvement. Thirdly, managers may believe that the perceived increase in commitment shown by workers results directly from employee share ownership and may promote further formal participation to enhance this development. And fourthly, employee share ownership may occasion increased delegation of authority at all levels in the organization.

Further evidence (Rosen, Klein and Young, 1985) also confirms Long's emphasis on the importance of management's philosophical commitment to share ownership in significantly enhancing the effects of profit-sharing and share-ownership schemes with regard to employee involvement and commitment to the company. Moreover, it should be stressed that the effectiveness of profit-sharing and share-ownership schemes may have more to do with managerial philosophy and style than with the level of share ownership *per se* (see also, Richardson and Nejad, 1986; Poole, 1988).

Organizational identity

A further argument in the literature relates to organizational identity and to instrumental attachments to work. It is hypothesized that when employees become shareholders they will have a further financial incentive to increase the worth of their share investment. This form of incentive has advantages over other forms in that, although indirect, it is thought to be long term and self-reinforcing (Copeman *et al*, 1984). Moreover, financial incentives are considered to be more effective when linked with ownership and, inasmuch as share ownership increases the employee's financial stake in his/her place of work, it also increases the instrumental importance of work. Thus, employee shareholders may be even more inclined to direct their individual and collective behaviour towards the corporate goal of increased profits rather than to the traditional worker's goal of higher wages and improved conditions of work (Meade, 1964; Copeman, 1976; Copeman *et al*, 1984; Bradley and Gelb, 1983b).

However, employee share-ownership schemes involve more than just the reward/effort relationship. Employees who participate in these schemes can now be clearly identified in a fundamental way with other shareholders through their common investment in the firm. More than this, the schemes, in changing the employee's status from one of 'employee' to 'owner' can occasion a link between employee interests and the interests of shareholders and the company (Nichols, 1964: 77–9; Wigham, 1973: 128; Ramsay and Haworth, 1984). Thus, in contrast with cash-based schemes, share-based arrangements (while also appealing to employees' instrumental orientations) purport to create a moral commitment to work and organizational goals and to effect substantial changes in employee attitudes and behaviour by creating a broader 'ownership identity' amongst employees generally (Long, 1981: 851). The identity with the company is encouraged by increased communications between management and the employee share-holder over and above that of the ordinary employee. Thus, employee shareholders receive the company's annual financial report and other shareholder information in addition to existing disclosure of information arrangements in the company (whether through management's own initiatives or through collective bargaining). Regardless of the employee's competence to evaluate such information, this involves an increase in communication of the financial status of the company and of important company policy. And, as such, it is scarcely surprising that Bell and Hanson (1984, 1987) have reported high levels of support by employees for profit sharing in principle and for company schemes and an increased interest in the profits and financial results of the company. Indeed, nearly a half of the respondents (47 per cent) said their loyalty to the firm had been strengthened and just over half (51 per cent) felt that the schemes made people work more effectively (Bell and Hanson, 1984, 1987; see also Fogarty and White, 1988).

In sum, it is thought that the combination of these factors may occasion an identification of employees with the firm and the products it produces. Indeed, the increased employee identification and commitment to the company and the enhanced interest in work may also influence either prospective employees to join, or existing employees to remain with, the company itself (Webb and Webb, 1897; Copeman and Rumble, 1972).

Employee satisfaction and commitment

But does the introduction of profit-sharing and share-ownership schemes transform employee attitudes? So far as employee satisfaction is concerned, there are thought to be at least two ways in which this may be improved through share ownership. First of all share ownership may directly affect employee satisfaction in the sense that ownership itself confers benefits on employees (such as, increased financial rewards). Secondly, it may indirectly affect employee satisfaction by increasing employee influence and involvement (Long, 1978a).

Turning to the actual evidence, Long (1978a and b) and Hammer, Stern and Gurdon (1982) have found positive relationships between employee ownership and employee satisfaction in individual firms. Also, a larger and more recent study by Rosen and Klein (1983) suggests that under the right conditions, employee share ownership can lead to increased employee satisfaction. However, other American studies have reported no significant difference in employee satisfaction between employee shareholders and non-shareholders (Hammer, Landau and Stern, 1981; French and Rosenstein, 1984).

The different findings may stem in part from the likelihood that satisfaction and commitment will be significantly influenced by the size of the company's contribution to the schemes (the amount of shares the participants receive and management's philosophical commitment to worker ownership). This would suggest that employees may regard the company's financial contribution as an important element in improving their morale and satisfaction at work (Rosen, Klein and Young, 1985). Other findings also suggest that the number of shares employees own, and the value of these shares, has some bearing on the perceived need for greater participation and control. Indeed, in Hochner and Granrose's (1983) study of a proposed employee buyout, employees highlighted entrepreneurship (financial gain being prominent) and participation as the major benefits of employee ownership.

Satisfaction may also stem from improved financial benefits. Thus, in Long's (1978a) study, employees felt that the advantages of employee ownership were in order of preference: financial gain; the satisfaction of working for oneself; greater influence in decision-making; a chance to benefit from one's own efforts; and, better understanding between management and employees. And Rosen and Klein (1986) concluded that employees are primarily motivated and inspired by the potential financial rewards of the schemes than any other factor. More generally, too, there is evidence from other than North American sources that employees' perceptions of the benefits of schemes arise from instrumental orientations to share schemes. Goldstein's (1978) West Australian study suggests that improvements in overall satisfaction, commitment, application (effort) and responsibility are positively related to the economic performance of the company. As a consequence, employee share ownership is viable only so long as the company can maintain a reasonable level of performance. (For other supporting evidence of the importance of employees' instrumental orientations to share schemes see Hammer and Stern, 1980; Greenberg, 1980; Rhodes and Steers, 1981; Rosen, Klein and Young, 1985.)

In short, the impact of employee share ownership on worker satisfaction links any improvements here to both the financial rewards of share ownership and to the possibility of enhanced employee participation. Moreover, what is clear is that there is an instrumental motivation of workers in becoming shareholders. However, this instrumentalism may take different forms such as protecting one's job, one's sole source of income (Stern and Hammer, 1978), or increasing financial awareness (French and Rosenstein, 1984).

Attitudes to the employment relationship

A final potential consequence of employee financial participation is that a change will be effected in employee attitudes to work, career and to social class relationships more generally. Not only is it hypothesized that employees will be more committed to productive efforts (see the section on the micro-economic impact of schemes) but also that they will wish to remain with the company and hence develop an organizational, rather than an individual, career commitment (for relevant studies see Long 1978b, 1980; Russell, Hochner and Perry, 1979; Hammer, Stern and Gurdon, 1982; French and Rosenstein, 1984).

Above all, it is argued that possession of shares means that the employee owns productive wealth and a part of the means of production. Against this, however, the employee's occupational position and his or her placement in the division of labour remain unchanged. Thus, employee shareholders differ theoretically in their class position from both ordinary employees and larger scale owners of capital. They occupy an ambiguous class position in that participants in share ownership schemes own the means of production, sell their labour power to others and do not directly control the work of others. However, share ownership may not only make the worker more sympathetic with the institution of private property (Copeman, Moore and Arrowsmith, 1984) but also raise both material and intrinsic expectations (Goldstein, 1978). Paradoxically, this in turn may result in greater dissatisfaction at work and possibly increased industrial conflict if employers fail to meet these new expectations (Rothschild-Whitt and Whitt, 1986).

Chapter two

A model and company economic and financial performance

So far, then, we have seen that profit-sharing and employee-shareholding schemes (together with developments in economic democracy more generally) have been advocated from a variety of standpoints. Indeed, economic, industrial relations and organizational arguments have all been marshalled to support the introduction of schemes. However, we have also noted that research findings on the impact of schemes are not consistent and while, on balance, they indicate some improvements in performance are likely to stem from the adoption of schemes, the effects would appear to fall substantially short of some of the more sweeping claims of the more ardent proponents of these practices.

At this juncture it is thus appropriate to examine in more depth and detail the impact of schemes based on the research findings of the Department of Employment project. We cannot of course use the data to test all the arguments which have been advanced in support of profit sharing (and, in particular, the macro-economic case is largely ignored). But the research material does allow a range of interesting and original findings to be brought to bear on the discussions on: (1) the economic and financial performance of companies; (2) the industrial relations implications of the introduction of schemes; and (3) organizational performance. Details of the methods used and the types of data available are set out in Appendix one.

This chapter begins with a research model to link theories and data. This is followed by an analysis of the impact of profit-sharing and employee-shareholding schemes on the financial performance of companies.

International research models

In the growing international literature on employee financial participation, a wide variety of models have been constructed that are based on different research objectives and assumptions.

In the USA, writers such as Hammer and Stern (1980), French (1987) and Pierce, Rubenfeld and Morgan (1988) have attempted to construct frameworks of profit sharing and its effects by focusing on a variety of instances at individual, group and company levels. By contrast, in Canada, in a series of articles, Long (1979, 1980a, 1980b, 1982), has concentrated on discovering those factors that moderate the relationship between employee ownership and predicted outcomes at the level of the firm. More specifically, in Long's influential conceptual framework (1978a), the idea of organizational identification is viewed as being based on three interrelated phenomena: integration, involvement and commitment. Following Argyris (1964), integration generally refers to the individual's perception of shared interests and goals with other members of the organization and in particular vertical integration. It is deemed to influence organizational performance by enhancing job effort and cooperation. Involvement is defined as a feeling of solidarity, a feeling of membership or belongingness. Involvement is hypothesized to be particularly apparent in three highlighted consequences of employee share ownership. These are: (a) that share acquisition leads to greater association with the firm; (b) that communications are increased in that additional company information is provided to the employee; and (c) that indirect involvement arises through integration. Further, in Australia, Goldstein (1978) has formulated a model of employee shareholder motivation linked with attitudinal responses at the level of the firm. Above all, based on the work of Vroom (1964), Goldstein has highlighted two major motivational factors or orientations resulting from employee share ownership; economic gain and intrinsic arousal.

A model for this research

For our part, the main elements of a research model on the impact of profit-sharing and employee-shareholding schemes are set out in Figure 2.1. The adoption of profit sharing and employee share-holding is seen to encourage greater organizational identification. This may occur from higher levels of either intrinsic or extrinsic commitment. Intrinsic commitment arises from greater direct participation, security, status and job satisfaction. Extrinisic commitment potentially stems from instrumental rewards, opportunistic gains or long-term investment advantages.

The main outcomes for companies are identified in terms of improved financial, industrial relations and organizational performance. Financial performance includes high levels of profitability and productivity. Industrial relations performance is associated with reduced conflict and lower levels of absenteeism

Figure 2.1 The impact of profit-sharing and employee-shareholding schemes

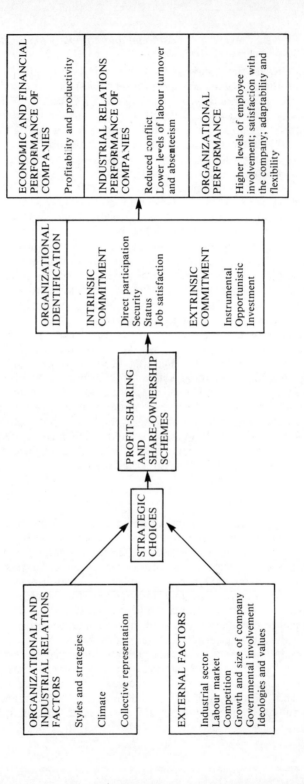

ORGANIZATIONAL AND INDUSTRIAL RELATIONS FACTORS

Styles and strategies

Climate

Collective representation

EXTERNAL FACTORS

Industrial sector
Labour market
Competition
Growth and size of company
Governmental involvement
Ideologies and values

STRATEGIC CHOICES

PROFIT-SHARING AND SHARE-OWNERSHIP SCHEMES

ORGANIZATIONAL IDENTIFICATION

INTRINSIC COMMITMENT

Direct participation
Security
Status
Job satisfaction

EXTRINSIC COMMITMENT

Instrumental
Opportunistic
Investment

ECONOMIC AND FINANCIAL PERFORMANCE OF COMPANIES

Profitability and productivity

INDUSTRIAL RELATIONS PERFORMANCE OF COMPANIES

Reduced conflict
Lower levels of labour turnover and absenteeism

ORGANIZATIONAL PERFORMANCE

Higher levels of employee involvement; satisfaction with the company; adaptability and flexibility and labour turnover. And improvements in organizational performance include higher levels of employee involvement, greater job satisfaction, and adaptability and flexibility.

The model also accommodates the central arguments set out in Volume 1 on the origins of profit-sharing and share-ownership schemes. It thus relates the adoption of employee financial participation to strategic choices linked with organizational and industrial relations factors and external, environmental variables. Moreover, it suggests that improvements in company performance are likely to have a positive 'feedback' influence that can, in turn, affect the broader context in which decisions to establish schemes are formulated.

Impact on company financial performance

Turning, then, to examine the impact of profit-sharing and share-ownership schemes on the economic and financial performance of companies, we have seen that the findings to date are not wholly consistent. This is partly because the relationship between profit-sharing and share-ownership schemes and economic performance may be influenced by other variables (such as employee attitudes to work, managerial performance and a company's financial commitment to schemes). And it is almost certainly the case that a company's pre-existing propensity to perform well is a major influence on company economic and financial performance rather than the introduction of schemes themselves. In other words, as we have argued, profit-sharing companies may not necessarily perform better *because* they have profit-sharing schemes, but because they are successful companies which consider that they should be involved in the sharing of this success with their employees.

The data presented below undoubtedly point to the tendency for a company to perform well to be a crucial variable in the adoption of schemes and in their continuing development (see also Goldstein, 1978). Moreover, although we are aware of the problems of generalizing from such data, we feel that the findings presented here are typical of the responses from all of the companies we studied. We begin by presenting evidence from the survey stage of the research on the perceived success of schemes. This is followed by data from the case study phase on the views of key respondents and employees concerning their impact of profit-sharing and share-ownership schemes on company economic and financial performance. We then analyse in more detail the relationship between profit sharing and share ownership and company performance in five companies, one from each industrial sector studied.

The impact of economic democracy

Survey data

In the survey stage of the research, a clear link between company growth and financial turnover on the one hand and the adoption of profit-sharing schemes was established (see Volume 1). Further information was also obtained on the perceived success of schemes, the results of which are set out in Table 2.1. Data are presented of success ratings using objectives of schemes considered to be very or fairly important in establishing a type of arrangement. It will be seen that Approved Profit Sharing (APS) schemes in particular were regarded as fairly successful as a tax efficient reward (for both company and employee), for ensuring a greater profit consciousness amongst employees and for resulting in employees benefiting from company profitability. However, the impact of schemes as an incentive for greater profitability and for increasing employees' understanding of financial issues were perceived to be far more restricted.

Table 2.1 Perceived success of schemes: survey stage of research

Success on different objectives	Type of scheme			
	APS	*SAYE*	*Other share*	*Cash*
To make employees feel they are part of the company	4.0	3.6	4.0	3.3
To make employees more profit conscious	4.0	3.7	3.5	4.2
To increase sense of commitment to the company	3.7	3.3	3.6	3.5
To ensure that employees benefit from company profitability	4.2	3.9	3.6	4.5
Tax efficient means of reward to employees	4.5	4.3	—	—
Incentive for greater productivity	3.3	3.1	3.2	3.2
To increase sense of respect between management and workforce	3.8	3.4	3.0	3.2
To increase employees' understanding of financial issues	3.1	3.2	3.3	3.3
Tax efficient means of reward for company	4.3	4.0	—	—

Note: Mean success ratings on a scale 5 to 1 (5 = very successful) of objectives rated as very/fairly important.

Key respondents' views

Turning more specifically to the case study data, our interviews with key respondents reinforced and amplified these findings. Indeed, a number of respondents argued that, in their view, profits were affected by forces over which the ordinary employee had virtually no control. Profits were seen to stem either from the sound policies and judgements of top executives (and hence the favourable assessment of Executive Share Option (ESO) schemes for this level of employee), or from a series of external environmental movements over which most organization members had no real influence. Forces of significance cited by the respondents include exchange rate movements, oil prices and the behaviour of foreign subsidiaries. Indeed, at one extreme, as the company secretary of an oil exploration company noted, 'In this business, profit sharing and share ownership can have *no* real effect on profitability'. Above all, key respondents noted considerable problems in measuring any direct consequences of schemes on profitability, because there are inevitably many other influences of potential consequences here. So far as the main types of schemes are concerned, ESO schemes, and to a lesser degree APS schemes, were seen to be the most likely to impact upon profitability. As we have noted, this applied especially to ESO schemes because of their potential consequences for the behaviour of senior executives. APS schemes were also perceived as potentially, if indirectly, valuable because they could serve to reduce labour turnover amongst competent staff who were difficult to replace.

At this juncture, it is also worth recalling the survey stage findings on trends in the workforce, where 67 per cent of firms with only APS schemes had experienced increases in employment in the last four years. This contrasted markedly with firms with only Save As You Earn (SAYE) schemes, where 35 per cent of companies had witnessed increases in the workforce (and 52 per cent had experienced a decrease). Given that SAYE schemes are particularly linked with the industrial relations policies of companies, it is scarcely surprising that any impact of these schemes on profitability was seen as typically indirect. Managers in finance departments appeared to be more hopeful that the schemes would impact upon profitability than their colleagues in personnel functions. But the very qualified views of key respondents in this respect should be stressed.

Employee attitudes

We were further aware from past research that the perceived employee rewards and company financial commitment to profit-sharing and share-ownership schemes could be vital components if schemes were to have a positive impact on company economic performance. In our survey of employee attitudes in the case study phase, we first asked respondents to what extent they favoured four main types of scheme: (1) profit-sharing (with cash rewards); (2) profit-sharing (through shares in the company); (3) Save As You Earn share option schemes; and (4) Executive share schemes.

The results are set out in Table 2.2 where it will be seen that, for the most part, there is a high level of commitment to schemes in principle. This applies particularly to profit sharing with cash awards. But there is also overwhelming support for share-based profit sharing and Save As You Earn schemes. The only exception is provided by the Executive Share Option schemes. It would be incorrect to suggest that employees typically oppose these types of arrangement but the most common response was one of indifference. Moreover, the negative and positive responses are roughly balanced.

There is little doubt, then, that proponents of all-employee profit-sharing and share-ownership schemes are attempting to introduce practices which are welcomed by the vast majority of the company's personnel. Notwithstanding a preference for cash-based arrangements, managements introducing schemes can be fairly secure in the knowledge that most types of profit sharing and share ownership will be welcomed by a substantial majority of employees.

We then asked respondents to indicate to what extent their company's schemes had been satisfactory in terms of rewards and who they felt were the main beneficiaries of such schemes. As will be seen in Table 2.3 there was in each case (APS, SAYE, ESO) a balance of positive over negative responses and, in particular, SAYE share ownership schemes were deemed satisfactory by a majority of employees. However, respondents, when asked who had benefited most from the schemes (workers, managers, undecided, both equally and other groups), considered managers to be the main beneficiaries of the schemes (see Table 2.4).

More specifically, we assessed employees' perceptions of the impact of profit-sharing and share-ownership schemes by obtaining employee estimates (on five point scales, from very successful to not at all successful) of the success of schemes in terms of a number of economic objectives. The largest single group of employees, as shown in Table 2.5, indicated in each case that the schemes had

Table 2.2 Employees' attitudes to profit-sharing and share-ownership schemes in general

Types of scheme	Strongly in favour 1	In favour 2	Neither in favour nor against 3	Against 4	Strongly against 5	No response	Mean	Standard deviation
1 Profit-sharing (with cash awards)	45	42	7	2	1	3	1.7	0.7
2 Profit-sharing (through shares in the company)	37	43	12	3	2	3	1.9	0.9
3 Save As You Earn share-ownership schemes	25	37	27	5	2	5	2.2	1.0
4 Executive share schemes	8	17	34	11	8	22	3.0	1.1

Note: Percentages, n = 1931.

Table 2.3 Employees' assessments of own company schemes in terms of rewards for employees

	Highly satisfactory			Highly unsatisfactory		Other/not applicable	Mean	SD
	1	2	3	4	5			
Profit-sharing (ADST)	7	41	20	19	8	6	2.8	1.1
Share-ownership (SAYE)	10	42	25	6	2	16	2.4	0.9
Executive share option (ESO)	5	15	33	5	5	37	2.9	1.0

Note: Percentages, n = 1931.

Table 2.4 Employees' views on principal beneficiaries of schemes

Main beneficiaries	
Workers	5
Managers	41
Undecided	18
Both equally	31
Other	4

Note: Percentage, n = 1931.

been unsuccessful in making employees more profit conscious/ more interested in the company's success; providing for a more efficient means of reward for employees and the company and ensuring that the employees benefit from the company's profitability. However, in the majority of instances, schemes were typically judged to have been neither successful nor unsuccessful. This applies to acting as an incentive to greater productivity, helping to hold down wage claims and increasing employees' understanding of the financial rewards of the company.

In order to assess the strength of significance of these data and their links/views on profit-sharing schemes factor analysis was employed. It will be seen from Table 2.6 that two factors were isolated that referred to financial incentives and financial rewards respectively.

In the first factor (financial incentives), highly significant relationships were found between attitudes to each scheme and making employees more profit conscious/more interested in the company's success and increasing the sense of cooperation between management and workforce. However, the relationship was much stronger for share-based schemes. This would suggest that positive attitudes to profit-sharing and share-ownership schemes, but particularly share-based schemes, leads to an identification with company goals and improved management/employee relations. Moreover, share-based schemes were also found to be similarly associated with increasing employees' sense of commitment to the company/making staff more likely to stay, acting as an incentive for greater productivity, making employees feel they are a part of the company and increasing employees' understanding of the financial issues that face the company. The exception was the association of schemes with helping to hold down wage claims, though this had a significant but weak association with executive share option schemes. Again, significant but weak associations were found between attitudes to cash-based schemes and making employees feel they are a part of the company and increasing

Table 2.5 Employees' estimates of the success of schemes in terms of a number of objectives

Objectives	Very successful	Successful	Neither successful nor unsuccessful	Unsuccessful	Not at all successful	Don't know	No response	Mean	SD
	1	2	3	4	5				
1 To make employees more profit conscious/more interested in the company's success	2	6	26	53	7	4	3	6	0.8
2 To increase employees' sense of commitment to the company/ make staff more liable to stay	4	10	42	33	4	4	3	2	0.9
3 Act as an incentive to greater productivity	3	11	47	29	3	3	3	2	0.8
4 To make employees feel that they are part of a company – working *with* it, not just *for* it	5	11	38	36	5	3	3	3	0.9
5 To help to hold down wage claims	7	20	42	8	3	7	14	2.7	0.9
6 To provide a tax efficient means of reward									
for employees	4	8	29	38	7	10	3	3.4	0.9
for company	2	4	27	34	11	17	6	3.6	0.9
7 To ensure that employees benefit from the company's profitability	4	8	22	52	6	4	4	3.5	0.9
8 To increase employees' understanding of the financial issues that face the company	5	13	39	32	3	5	4	3.2	0.9
9 To increase the sense of cooperation between management and workforce	7	16	51	17	2	4	4	2.9	0.9

Note: Percentages. N = 1031

Table 2.6 Employee attitudes to success of schemes and profit sharing or share ownership

	Profit sharing (cash)	Profit sharing (shares)	SAYE	Executive	Factor loadings
Factor 1 Financial incentives					
1 Make employees more profit conscious/more interested in the company's success	.08**	.25**	.20**	.21**	0.68
2 Increase employee's sense of commitment to the company/make staff more likely to stay	.05	.27**	.20**	.21**	0.81
3 Act as an incentive for greater productivity	.04	.23**	.17**	.23**	0.85
4 Make employees feel that they are a part of the company – working *with* it, not just *for* it	.07*	.27**	.17**	.23**	0.78
5 To help hold down wage claims	.02	.02	.01	.07*	0.42
9 To increase employees' understanding of the financial issues that face the company	.07*	.19**	.14**	.15**	0.53
10 To increase the sense of cooperation between management and workforce	.08**	.21**	.12**	.21**	0.67
Factor 2 Financial rewards					
6 To provide a tax efficient means of reward for the employees	.08**	.31**	.26**	.23**	0.85
7 To provide a tax efficient means of reward for the company	.08**	.18**	.16**	.11**	0.78
8 To ensure that the employees benefit from the company's profitability	.06	.31**	.22**	.24**	0.74

Notes: Pearson product moment correlation coefficients – two-tailed significance.
  * Significant at 0.01 level.
  ** Significant at 0.001 level.
  The two factors account for 60.9 per cent of the shared variance.

employees' understanding of the financial issues that face the company. Share-based schemes do appear, therefore, to provide a financial incentive to employees and have more of an impact on employee attitudes than cash-based schemes.

In the second factor (financial rewards), again the importance of share-based schemes can be noted. Highly significant relationships were discovered between views on share-based schemes and the adjudged success of schemes in providing a tax efficient means of reward for employees and for the company and in ensuring that employees benefit from company profitability. Although significant relationships were identified between cash-based schemes and providing a tax efficient means of reward for the employees and the company for most of the items weaker associations were found. Again, then, the relationship between financial rewards and share-based schemes appears to be much stronger than that for cash-based schemes, suggesting the advantages of share-type arrangements for developing an identification of employees with managerial goals and objectives in the company as a whole.

In summary, then, although employees in general did not consider that schemes had been particularly successful in achieving managerial objectives so far as financial performance is concerned, views on profit-sharing schemes in general were linked with their assessments. And certainly positive views on share-based schemes are interlinked with the view that profit sharing has enabled management to achieve a number of the financial objectives of the schemes themselves.

Individual company performance

The relationship between profit-sharing and share-ownership schemes and economic performance of the companies remains a central issue in much of the literature. One way of assessing this relationship is by detailed analysis of individual cases where the relationship between the adoption of schemes and their impact on economic performance can be more readily observed. In the case study stage, we therefore examined, where possible, each company's financial performance over a ten-year period on the basis of a number of indicators (annual profits after tax, annual turnover and sales, annual capital-labour ratio and annual earnings per share). Much of this information was provided by the companies themselves but, where necessary, information was gathered from existing published sources.

The analysis focuses on a single company within each industrial sector over a given period of time. More detailed comparative analysis of the data was not possible given that the data for each company may differ slightly in terms of accounting practices, rights issues, corporate reorganization and so on. These differences are less serious, however, if the analysis concentrates on individual companies over a given time period. Moreover, given that we are concerned with examining the relationship between the impact of individual schemes or a combination of profit-sharing and share-ownership schemes and company economic performance, case study material lends itself more readily to this mode of analysis. Furthermore, in each context, the data provides a valuable indicator of the relationship between profit-sharing and share-ownership schemes and economic performance.

Case 1: A finance sector company

The first case chosen is a finance sector company with a workforce of 2,800. The company had introduced an unapproved SAYE scheme in 1976 and had an unapproved ESO scheme running through from 1976 to 1984. An unapproved SAYE scheme was introduced in 1980, an approved ESO scheme in 1984 and an APS scheme in 1985. What impact, if any, can we infer this adoption of schemes had on economic performance?

On the basis of the accompanying evidence (Table 2.7), it would appear to be the case that while the unapproved schemes had little impact on company performance, the approved schemes had a far greater impact, and that this particularly applied to the positive consequences of the SAYE and ESO schemes. Certainly the trends in after tax profits, turnover and earnings per share are suggestive of such a relationship. Indeed, after tax profits in the company rose spectacularly and consistently from £9.7 million in 1980 to £33.5 million in 1985. Turnover over the same period was £49.2 million and £138.7 million respectively, with earnings per 12½p share rising from 5.97p to 20.05p.

However, following the adoption of the unapproved schemes in 1976, there followed a period of static or declining economic performance until 1980. Company performance then improved and was *accompanied* by the introduction of a SAYE scheme and an impressive performance followed throughout the 1980s. The fact that the earlier unapproved schemes had little impact on economic performance suggests that the *timing* of schemes may be crucial to company success. Moreover, it could also be argued that the upwardly rising trend in fortunes provided a positive setting for the development of ESO and APS schemes in the mid-1980s which appeared, if anything, to trigger further improvements in 1985–6.

The introduction of schemes in the 1980s thus helped to reinforce an already expanding business with an impressive performance on profits, turnover and earnings per share. Significantly, the relatively later introduction of an APS scheme was associated with the awareness of a potential loss of able personnel when it became clear to the company that many of their competitors were developing schemes. ESO schemes were seen as absolutely fundamental because key personnel who left the firm would typically take their clients with them. Hence, these had been set up in 1976 well before the 1984 Act and considerably prior to the substantial improvement in company profitability (which had been aided by the relaxation of exchange controls).

Table 2.7 A finance sector company

Year	Profit after tax £'000	Earnings* per 12½p share p	Turnover £'000	Capital/labour ratio
1976	7,869	4.71	32,900	
1977	8,788	5.46	37,450	
1978	8,691	5.42	41,410	
1979	8,058	5.07	44,356	
1980	9,683	5.97	49,210	
1981	13,421	8.08	60,276	
1982	15,659	9.47	74,577	23.9
1983	19,652	11.78	93,068	26.36
1984	24,419	14.61	115,927	29.92
1985	33,530	20.05	138,725	31.43

Note: * 1986 change in share value from 25p to 12½p.

1976–80	SAYE (NA)
1976–84	ESO (NA)
1980	SAYE
1984	ESO
1985	APS.

Case 2: A manufacturing company

This involved a large manufacturing concern with a workforce of over 57,000 employees. It had introduced an early profit-sharing scheme in 1954 and an unapproved SAYE scheme in 1979. In 1980, an APS scheme had been introduced followed by approved SAYE and ESO schemes in 1984. The adoption of profit-sharing and share-ownership schemes paralleled changing economic fortunes for the company in question. In 1979, the firm's after tax profits were a healthy £490 million but fell to £161 million in 1980 and

£167 million in 1982. A recovery in 1983 produced after tax profits of £418 million, £661 million in 1984 and £604 million in 1985 (Table 2.8). Also, earnings per £1 share slumped from 79.2p in 1979 to 22.1p in 1980 and remained relatively low until improvements in 1983 which produced earnings per share of 65.3p, 98.2p and 86.4p in 1983, 1984 and 1985. However, turnover from sales rose slowly for most of the period from £2,332 million in 1979 to £3,011 million in 1985.

The after tax profits and earnings per share in this company are thus dominated by an abrupt decline in 1979 and the early 1980s on which the existing schemes for profit sharing and share ownership had little impact. Again, reinforcing the importance of external factors, the decline is explicable almost entirely by the unfavourable exchange rate movements of the period and the consequences that these had for a large number of British firms in manufacturing industry (this is suggested further by the fact that turnover remained fairly satisfactory throughout the period).

Table 2.8 A manufacturing sector company

Year	Profit after tax £m	Earnings per £1 share p	Turnover (UK) £m	Capital/ labour ratio
1975	167	29.7	1,314	
1976	268	45.2	1,616	
1977	376	60.9	1,868	
1978	360	58.6	1,800	
1979	490	79.2	2,332	
1980	161	22.1	2,399	
1981	224	32.3	2,575	3.96
1982	167	24.2	2,848	4.54
1983 *	418	65.3	2,866	5.4
1984	661	98.2	3,131	6.53
1985	604	86.4	3,011	6.11

Note: 1954 — SAYE (NA); 1980 — APS; 1984 — SAYE, ESO.

The company met the crisis it experienced in profitability and earnings per share by a major restructuring exercise, by substantial redundancies and by increasing significantly the extent of its overseas investments. Its ability to carry out such a major organizational change was recognized as having been assisted by a good industrial relations climate (in which employee involvement generally was a prominent feature). However, profit sharing and share ownership was in no way an insurance against a major decline in profitability occasioned by the adverse external conditions cited above. On the contrary, the company had adopted both SAYE and APS schemes at the crucial period of its decline and arguably it awaited the economic recovery in 1983 before the introduction of the SAYE and ESO schemes in 1984.

Case 3: A service sector company

In the services sector, a large company with a rapidly expanding turnover and level of profitability was selected. The firm had concerns in hotels, entertainments, gambling and a variety of other leisure activities with over 20,000 employees in the UK. In 1979, it introduced an APS scheme followed by an approved SAYE scheme in 1983. An ESO scheme was set up earlier in 1971 and adopted in 1978 receiving approval from the Inland Revenue in 1984.

Although the APS scheme was introduced before the commencement of our series of economic indicators, the approved SAYE and ESO schemes came on stream against a background of consistently rising trends in after tax profits, turnover, capital-labour ratio and earnings per share (Table 2.9). Profits after tax were thus £32.5 million in 1981 rising to £75.1 million in 1985. Turnover in these two years was £705.6 million and £1,342.6 million and earnings per 10p share 24.3p and 35.57p.

Part of this impressive economic performance can be explained by considerable merger and takeover activity during the period in question. Significantly, the schemes were noted by the company secretary as being potentially valuable in defusing opposition from employees in firms that were being taken over. However, this case study again reinforces the view that profit-sharing and share-ownership schemes tend to accompany rather than occasion expansionary economic profiles.

Table 2.9 A service sector company

Year	Profit after tax £m	Earnings per 10p share p	Turnover £m	Capital labour ratio
1980			665.1	
1981	32.5	24.3	705.6	0.014
1982	35.4	23.5	762.0	0.014
1983	41.8	27.0	846.9	0.019
1984	50.2	28.6	1,115.9	0.027
1985	75.1	35.6	1,342.6	

Note: 1971 — ESO (NA); 1978–84 — ESO (NA); 1979 — APS; 1983 — SAYE; 1984 — ESO.

Case 4: A retail company

This company, though best known for its retailing activities also had a number of manufacturing units in which specialist goods were produced for its shops; it employed over 11,000 employees. The size of the company had grown considerably in the 1980s largely through merger activities. The commitment of the founder member of the company was crucial to the early development of the non-approved APS and ESO schemes in 1976. An approved APS scheme was developed in 1985 and an approved SAYE scheme was introduced in 1987.

Table 2.10 shows the spectacular rise in after tax profits, turnover and earnings per share: profits rising from £2.7 million in 1980 to £23.6 million in 1985, turnover from £58.2 million to £446.7 million and earnings per 10p share from 8.3p to 22.3p. However, the effects of merger will be noted in the varied (and, at times, declining) capital-labour ratio of the company.

Table 2.10 A retail sector company

Year	Profit after tax £'000	Earnings per 10p share p	Turnover £'000	Capital/ labour ratio
1980	2,699	8.3	58,213	4.46
1981	2,862	8.6	67,165	5.03
1982	6,823	9.9	157,147	13.35
1983	12,006	11.3	243,974	8.75
1984	19,224	18.2	375,410	8.21
1985	23,637	22.3	446,733	9.27
1986	34,743		476,917	

Note: 1976–9 – APS (NA); 1976–84 – ESO (NA); 1979 – APS; 1984 – ESO.

The impact of specific schemes, as in all these cases, is of course complicated by the variety of different schemes adopted at different times. There is some evidence to suggest that the earlier schemes had favourable affects on profitability and that the 1985 ESO schemes *followed* a period of spectacular performance. However, it is our contention that the relationship between schemes and this spectacular economic performance are less direct and that the substantial gains in turnover and profits were almost certainly reflections of good management, product design and marketing and the mergers which took place with other viable and expanding companies.

Case 5: An energy ('other') sector company

Our final case study is an oil exploration company with 122 employees. In 1980 the company adopted an approved APS scheme and a non-approved ESO scheme. These schemes were followed by an approved SAYE scheme in 1982 and by an approved ESO scheme in 1984.

The economic performance indicators for the company are interesting because of the fluctuations in profits, turnover and earnings per share during the time period covered. As can be seen from Table 2.11, after tax profits peaked at £41 million in 1981 (they were £36.2, £24.9, £31.6 and £37.7 million in 1982, 1983, 1984 and 1985 respectively). Turnover generally rose from £63.4 million in 1979 to £348 million in 1985 but there was a fall between 1982 (£241 million) and 1983 (£215.5 million). Earnings per share fluctuated but was higher in 1982 (36.7p per 25p share) than in 1985 (31.3p per 25p share). The company generally became more capital-intensive (it had a very low ratio anyway), though there were marginal falls between 1981−2 and 1983−4.

The adoption of schemes does not necessarily relate in any obvious way to these variations. The 1980 and 1984 schemes fit the view that successful economic performance is a precursor for the development of schemes. However, the 1982 SAYE scheme was developed when profitability and turnover were both sluggish and which actually declined in the six months to one year period following their adoption.

Table 2.11   An 'other' sector company

Year	Profit after tax £m	Earnings per 25p share p	Turnover £m	Capital labour ratio
1979	9.3		63.4	0.33
1980	22.0		108.4	0.51
1981	41.0		237.1	1.0
1982	36.2	36.7	241.0	0.96
1983	24.9	26.9	215.5	1.5
1984	31.6	30.3	263.4	1.44
1985	37.7	31.3	348.0	1.84

Note: 1980 − APS, ESO (NA); 1982 − SAYE; 1984 − ESO.

Conclusion

In sum there would appear to be a highly complex pattern so far as the relationship between profit-sharing and share-ownership schemes and the economic and financial performance of companies is concerned. Broadly, as others have discovered, there is a link between economic success and the adoption of profit-sharing and share-ownership schemes; but our specific case study data suggests that for the most part, this relationship is not necessarily in the direction sometimes proposed.

Our examination of the economic performance of the companies suggests that a favourable economic performance in the company often provides the basis for the adoption of schemes rather than the other way round. However, the introduction of schemes probably enables companies to continue with (and even enhance) a positive performance because there are then no potentially negative consequences of a company making substantial profits and not being prepared to ensure that some part of the increased surplus returns to the workforce. This would partly explain our findings in Volume 1, that 70 per cent of 303 'main stage' firms with all-employee schemes had experienced an increase in business volume compared with only 14 per cent which had witnessed a decrease. However, the complex interconnections between profit-sharing and share-ownership schemes on the economic and financial performance of companies should be stressed. There is almost certainly a positive and mutually reinforcing relationship. But the effects are often indirect and less marked than some of the proponents of profit sharing have advocated. And wider environmental influences (such as exchange rate movements, oil price movements and so on) can impact substantially on profitability as well.

Chapter three

Industrial relations performance

As we have seen, the anticipated benefits of profit sharing and share ownership are not confined to economic and financial issues alone. On the contrary, a strong case has been made for developing schemes on the grounds of their positive impact on industrial relations performance. To assess this further argument we begin with an analysis of behavioural data from the case studies. This is followed by an examination of the impact of schemes on trade unionism in the firm.

In the case study stage of the research reported here we attempted to examine the impact of schemes on such issues as strike activity, absenteeism and labour turnover. At the outset, it should be emphasized that the time series data available in many of the companies studied was typically far from adequate and sometimes simply not available at all. Indeed, the data presented here should be regarded as indicative of probable patterns rather than comprising the basis for definite conclusions so far as absenteeism and labour turnover are concerned. Instead of examining cases in different sectors, it proved feasible to focus on only manufacturing industry and to make some detailed comparisons between two contrasting companies in this particular sector. We begin, however, with an examination of the impact of employee ownership on strike activity.

Strikes

Industrial relations performance is an elusive concept and by no means easy to measure satisfactorily. Strikes are clearly one index, but in any given year the vast majority of companies in Britain and overseas do not have any serious stoppages of work of this type. It is thus hardly surprising that the bulk of the case study firms had been relatively free of stoppages. On the other hand, it is very difficult to conclude from out data that profit sharing and share ownership reduced strike propensity. Moreover, we do not have information on stoppages in the case study companies for the 1960s and much of the 1970s. However, in a firm in the distribution sector, a major stoppage occurred only a year after the adoption of a scheme. In a manufacturing concern, the specialist director of human resources policy and planning reported to us that, in the previous year, there had been a dispute at one site which had lasted for six weeks and involved 275 people.

The relationship between profit sharing or share ownership and strike activity is thus again complex. Amongst the many well managed firms which we visited and which had no recent strike experience, part of the explanation was probably the 'style' and approach adopted by managers to industrial relations generally. Moreover, some respondents did see the introduction of schemes as a part of their attempt to secure a good climate for industrial and employee relations. Yet, at best, schemes may be said to reduce disputes in a very modest way and largely as part of a much wider set of measures introduced by companies to create a positive atmosphere for employer–employee relationships as a whole.

Absenteeism and labour turnover

Other indices of industrial relations performance are absenteeism and labour turnover. However, few key respondents noted any marked direct improvement in behaviour in these respects following the introduction of schemes. This applied particularly to absenteeism rates. A typical response came from an insurance company where it was noted that, 'There is no firm link between absenteeism and the introduction of schemes, other external factors are more important.' For labour turnover the situation was a little different. One of the prescribed aims of profit-sharing and share-ownership schemes is to discourage labour turnover at least amongst senior and highly skilled staff. Moreover, the majority of firms which have profit-sharing and share-ownership arrangements limit participation in schemes to those employees who have been with the firm a while. And, of course, employees in some cases will lose financially if they leave the firms other than for such reasons as retirement or sickness.

Notwithstanding again the problems of measurement, many key respondents still noted that the characteristics of an industry, the levels of unemployment and so on were the most critical influences on labour turnover. For example, in a retailing firm, it was noted that there were inevitably high rates of turnover of staff and that the introduction of schemes could do no more than have a very

modest impact. The chief personnel officer of a large manufacturing concern also noted that, 'Share schemes can only have a
secondary effect on these factors and no direct effect. The overall
industrial relations policy is far more important'. On the other
hand, in some firms (especially in the finance sector) key
respondents did suggest that some improvements in labour turnover had occurred following the introduction of schemes. In sum,
when we asked key respondents – many of whom had invested a
considerable personal effort into the development of schemes – to
assess their actual impact on industrial relations performance, the
predominant view was that the relationship with absenteeism was
limited though some effects on labour turnover were anticipated.

To assess these judgements in more detail, we examined the rates
of absenteeism and labour turnover in the companies we visited.
The first of the two manufacturing firms which we chose to analyse
in more depth specializes in the production of fashion clothing. It
has a manufacturing site which we visited in the South East and
employs 7,700 people. It introduced APS and SAYE schemes in
1984 following an improvement in profits performance. In Table
3.1 the quarterly percentage absenteeism are set out. Essentially, it
will be seen that in the key year of 1984 absenteeism rates were
slightly higher than for the previous year. The 1985–6 figures show
no appreciable and consistently declining trend and despite an
improvement in the early part of the year, the overall percentage
rate of absenteeism was slightly higher in 1985 than in 1984 (6.25
per cent compared with 6.14 per cent).

Table 3.1 Manufacturing company (A)
Absenteeism: quarterly† percentages – 1979–86 (Site in South East)

Year	1979	1980	1981	1982	1983	1984	1985	1986
1	8.5	7.2	5.2	7.5	5.8	6.8	6.2	6.1
2	7.1	6.4	4.7	5.6	4.3	5.8	5.7	5.1*
3**	8.3	6.7	6.1	5.3	5.3	6.2	6.2	
4	6.4	5.2	6.4	4.9	5.8	5.7	6.9	
	7.6	6.4	5.6	5.8	5.3	6.1	6.3	5.7

Notes: † Every 13 weeks.
  * Only six weeks.
  ** Plant closes down for 4 weeks.

In the case of a larger manufacturing concern, the data provided
(see Table 3.2) was on an annual basis and covered male absenteeism rates for the group as a whole rather than for a single site. The
main feature of the series is the consistently declining rate of

absenteeism from 1980 (6.67 per cent) to 1984 (5.84 per cent) following a slight increase between 1976 (7.51 per cent) and 1979 (7.65 per cent). Some of the company's schemes for employee financial participation were introduced well before 1979 and the 1984 schemes appear to have had no effect on absenteeism in the company at all (5.84 per cent, 1984; 5.85 per cent, 1985). Indeed, it is almost certain that the recession in manufacturing largely explained the overall patterns.

Table 3.2 Manufacturing company (B)
Absenteeism: annual percentages for the company as a whole (Male employees)

Year	1976	1977	1978	1979	1980	1981	1982	1983	1984	1985
Male absenteeism rate	7.5	7.5	7.6	7.7	6.7	6.7	6.2	5.8	5.8	5.9

Table 3.3 Manufacturing company (A)
Labour turnover*: quarterly† percentages – 1976–86 (Site in South East)

Year	1975	1976	1977	1978	1979	1980	1981	1982	1983	1984	1985	1986
1	4.2	2.8	3.6	3.7	4.8	4.1	1.1	1.8	3.0	2.8	2.9	3.5
2	4.2	3.4	3.7	4.0	4.9	3.4	1.5	2.3	2.2	1.7	3.3	
3	4.1	4.0	4.1	3.8	5.6	3.1	1.9	2.4	2.6	2.4	3.9	
4	2.4	2.7	4.1	3.6	4.6	2.0	1.4	1.1	2.0	2.2	3.7	
	3.7	3.2	3.9	3.8	5.0	3.1	1.5	1.9	2.4	2.3	3.4	

Notes: † Every 3 months.
    * Formula used: leavers in month × 100 ÷ number employed.

In some ways, however, the labour turnover rates are the more important set of statistics. After all, key managers generally appreciated that any consequences of schemes for absenteeism were likely to be indirect and difficult to quantify. Yet, in some cases, there was hope expressed that profit sharing and share ownership could increase loyalty and reduce labour turnover rates.

From the data available from the fashion clothing manufacturer, however, there is little evidence to suggest that share-based profit sharing has any marked impact on labour turnover rates (see Table 3.3). Indeed, taking the key date of 1984 (*ie* when the APS and SAYE schemes were introduced), the annual labour turnover rate (excluding redundancies) rose in the year following the introduction of schemes (2.27 per cent in 1984; 3.42 per cent in 1985).

The large manufacturing company had far more fluctuating rates of labour turnover (the uncertainties occasioned by a major

The impact of economic democracy

restructuring exercise were almost certainly in part responsible). However, as Table 3.4 indicates, the introduction of an unapproved ESO scheme in 1979 and an approved APS scheme in 1980 had no obvious effect on this situation at all. Labour turnover (excluding redundancies) was 11.6 per cent in 1980 and 14.0 per cent in 1981. In short, our data suggest that labour turnover is influenced particularly by economic and organizational changes which are of greater consequence than the impact of profit-sharing and share-ownership schemes. The adoption of schemes may have some relationship with outcomes and they can certainly prevent a movement away from a given company to a competitor *with* schemes. But, as this comparison shows, profit-sharing and share-ownership schemes do not necessarily have far reaching implications for either labour turnover or absenteeism. Furthermore, they do not appear to counter in any major way the effects of other much more fundamental forces which impact on these aspects of industrial relations.

Table 3.4 Manufacturing company (B)
Annual percentage labour turnover for the company as a whole* (Male employees)

Year	1976	1977	1978	1979	1980	1981	1982	1983	1984	1985
Labour turnover	8.2	9.7	8.7	9.0	11.6	14.0	7.1	12.7	6.7	Not available

Note: * Formula used: leavers in year × 100 ÷ number employed.

Trade unions

A longstanding objective of profit sharing has of course been to reduce conflict between trade unions and management in the firm. However, there is little detailed evidence available on the precise impact of schemes on trade unionism. In Volume 1, we noted that there was a positive relationship between the existence of trade unions in the firm and the presence of one or more of the various types of all-employee schemes for profit sharing and share owner-ship. In the case study stage, following Long (1979), we attempted to measure in more detail the differing patterns of relationships between share ownership in the employing company and attitudes of employees, trade unionists and non-trade unionists to trade unions. Similarly, we also endeavoured to analyse the relationships that exist between share ownership in the employing company and the attitudes of trade unionists and non-trade unionists to the schemes themselves.

Table 3.5 Employees' attitudes to trade unions by company share-owner-ship status

| | Shareholders N = 377 | | Non-shareholders N = 253 | | |
	Mean	SD	Mean	SD	t
Basically, the union and management have similar goals	3.23	1.72	3.21	1.50	0.15
It is difficult to be loyal to the company *and* to the union	3.89	1.72	3.89	1.69	0.00
†A union is really necessary in this firm at this time	5.61	1.66	5.43	1.70	− 1.31
There is no reason why the union and management cannot work together	5.63	1.19	5.19	1.33	4.16****
Without a union, employees would probably not get fair treatment from management	4.92	1.83	5.02	1.66	− 0.73
The union works primarily for the best interests of its members	5.23	1.47	5.31	1.29	− 0.76
The best way of obtaining worker say or influence in decision-making in this firm is through increasing the influence of the union	4.03	1.82	4.44	1.61	− 2.98***

Notes: †This item has been reversed so that a higher numerical value indicates a higher perceived need for the union.
* = p 0.10, two-tailed.
** = p 0.05, two-tailed.
*** = p 0.01, two-tailed.
**** = p 0.001, two-tailed.

Table 3.5 sets out data from the unionized case study companies and entails a comparison between employee shareholders and non-shareholders. The relatively large number of employee share-holders stems from including participants in any type of scheme (APS, SAYE, other share-based). The table shows for the most part a similar set of attitudes of employee shareholders and non-shareholders. Where there are significant differences is in attitudes to union-management cooperation and the role of the union in decision-making. Employee shareholders generally feel more strongly that unions and managements should be able to work together and are more ambivalent with respect to the decision-making role of trade unions than that of non-shareholders. In short, although there are few significant differences between these two groups of respondent, it does appear that employee shareholders are particularly liable to stress that union–management relationships should be non-conflictual and are more prone than non-shareholders to emphasize that channels other than that of the union are the best way of obtaining a greater decision-making influence for the workforce as a whole. This does suggest that a modest change in the climate of industrial relations stems from employee shareholding, though it may be, of course, that employees with such views are more likely to avail themselves of the opportunities to participate in share-based schemes in the first place. However, the strategy of management of deploying SAYE and other share-based schemes to improve industrial relations does appear to have been at least partially successful so far as employee attitudes are concerned.

It could be objected that a better test of the impact of schemes on industrial relations is to contrast the views of trade-unionists and non-trade-unionists, and to link these with ownership or non-ownership of shares in the company. In Table 3.6, trade-unionists' attitudes to trade unionism are thus broken down by share owner-ship. The data reinforce the arguments above since there are relatively few significant differences between these two groups of respondents. However, the employee shareholders amongst the trade unionists in our sample are more likely to stress cooperative management–union relationships and are less likely than non-shareholders to view the union as the best way of obtaining greater worker influence over decision-making in the firm.

There is no doubt, too, that the influence of share ownership on non-trade-unionists' attitudes in unionized firms is a significant factor affecting the views on trade unions as a whole. The relevant data are set out in Table 3.7 where it will be seen that the non-unionist employee shareholders are more likely to emphasize the similarity in union and management goals; to stress the potentially cooperative nature of relationships between unions and manage-ment; to reject the view that, without unionism, employees would probably not get fair treatment from management; and to indicate that the union element of representation is not necessarily the most appropriate way of obtaining a greater worker influence over decision-making in the company.

In sum, our data suggest that there is probably an impact of the

Table 3.6 Trade unionists' attitudes to trade unions by company share-ownership status

	Shareholders N = 262		Non-shareholders N = 167		
	Mean	*SD*	*Mean*	*SD*	*t*
Basically, the union and management have similar goals	3.23	1.72	3.40	1.57	− 1.04
It is difficult to be loyal to the company *and* to the union	3.70	1.67	3.92	1.73	− 1.29
†A union is really necessary in this firm at this time	6.11	1.24	5.84	1.53	− 1.89*
There is no reason why the union and management cannot work together	5.65	1.14	5.28	1.38	2.92***
Without a union, employees would probably not get fair treatment from management	5.42	1.52	5.37	1.53	0.32
The union works primarily for the best interests of its members	5.37	1.29	5.48	1.23	− 0.88
The best way of obtaining worker say or influence in decision-making in this firm is through increasing the influence of the union	4.41	1.72	4.78	1.54	− 2.33**

Notes: †This item has been reversed so that a higher numerical value indicates a higher perceived need for the union.
  * = p 0.10, two-tailed.
  ** = p 0.05, two-tailed.
  *** = p 0.01, two-tailed.

introduction of share-based schemes on attitudes to trade unionism. In most cases, this is not strong, but it is likely that schemes will improve the attitudinal climate of industrial relations to at least a modest extent. Moreover, the greatest impact would appear to be amongst non-trade unionists in unionized firms who are likely to emphasize that a relatively cooperative and non-conflictual mode of relationship between unions and management in the firm is appropriate.

Table 3.7 Non-trade unionists' attitudes to trade unions by company share-ownership status

	Shareholders N = 110		Non-shareholders N = 85		
	Mean	SD	Mean	SD	t
Basically, the union and management have similar goals	3.26	1.73	2.82	1.27	2.01**
It is difficult to be loyal to the company *and* to the union	4.28	1.74	3.85	1.61	1.81*
†A union is really necessary in this firm at this time	4.42	1.91	4.62	1.73	0.79
There is no reason why the union and management cannot work together	5.55	1.29	5.07	1.19	2.71***
Without a union, employees would probably not get fair treatment from management	3.71	1.95	4.37	1.70	−2.50**
The union works primarily for the best interests of its members	4.85	1.79	4.98	1.36	−0.58*
The best way of obtaining worker say or influence in decision-making in this firm is through increasing the influence of the union	3.11	1.71	3.78	1.55	−2.85***

Notes: †This item has been reversed so that a higher numerical value indicates a higher perceived need for the union.
* = p 0.10, two-tailed.
** = p 0.05, two-tailed.
*** = p 0.01, two-tailed.

No study involving an assessment of attitudes to profit-sharing and employee-shareholding schemes would be complete, however, without some reference to the views of trade unionists and non-trade unionists respectively on actual schemes. Thus, in Table 3.8, trade unionists' attitudes to profit-sharing and share-ownership schemes are presented. As is to be expected, employee shareholder trade unionists are shown to be less in favour of cash-based profit-sharing schemes than non-shareholding trade unionists. Again,

Table 3.8 Trade unionists' support for profit-sharing and share-owner-ship schemes by company share ownership

	Shareholders N = 308		Non-shareholders N = 146		
	Mean	SD	Mean	SD	t
Profit sharing (cash)	1.82	0.81	1.58	0.72	3.08***
Profit sharing (shares)	2.00	0.96	2.28	0.89	−3.03***
SAYE	2.11	0.99	2.49	0.86	−4.16****
Executive	3.18	1.22	3.02	0.87	1.62

Notes: * = p 0.10, two-tailed.
** = p 0.05, two-tailed.
*** = p 0.01, two-tailed.
**** = p 0.001, two-tailed.

shareholding trade union members have a particular propensity to favour share-based profit-sharing and SAYE schemes.

These findings are amplified in Table 3.9, which presents data on non-trade unionists' attitudes to profit-sharing and share-owner-ship schemes. It will be seen that few significant differences in attitudes exist between shareholding and non-shareholding non-trade unionists to profit-sharing and share-ownership schemes. However, as is to be expected, employee shareholders who are not union members are more favourable to SAYE schemes than their colleagues who hold no shares in their employing organization.

Table 3.9 Non-trade unionists' support for profit-sharing and share-ownership schemes by company share ownership

	Shareholders N = 84		Non-shareholders N = 74		
	Mean	SD	Mean	SD	t
Profit sharing (cash)	1.69	0.81	1.60	0.78	0.76
Profit sharing (shares)	1.83	0.94	2.00	0.74	−1.24
SAYE	1.89	0.93	2.41	0.91	−3.50****
Executive	2.86	1.30	2.97	0.92	−0.65

Notes: * = p .10, two-tailed.
** = p .05, two-tailed.
*** = p .01, two-tailed.
**** = p .001, two-tailed.

Furthermore, it is worth emphasizing that favourable attitudes to profit sharing and share ownership do appear to be related to views on unions and the company. Hence, we asked employees whether they considered the best representative of their interests to be the union or the company. As will be seen from Table 3.10, with the exception of cash-based arrangements, positive views on profit sharing undoubtedly appear to be related to a greater identification with the company rather than the union.

Table 3.10 Employee interests or attitudes to profit sharing or share ownership

	Profit sharing (cash)	Profit sharing (shares)	SAYE	Executive share option
The best representative of an employee's interests is the union not the company	− 0.07	− 0.19**	− 0.12**	− 0.25**

Notes: Pearson product moment correlation coefficients − two-tailed significance.
    * Significant at 0.01 level.
    ** Significant at 0.001 level.

Conclusion

So far as the impact of profit sharing and employee shareholding on industrial relations is concerned, then, a highly interesting set of conclusions emerges. Senior managerial personnel involved in the establishment of schemes indicated that they hoped to accomplish an improvement in the climate of union−management relations, but did not expect major changes in behaviour arising from schemes. Our behavioural and attitudinal data lend considerable support to their judgement in this respect. With the possible exception of labour turnover, few marked effects of schemes on industrial relations behaviour were observed. However, with respect to attitudes, employee shareholders were found to be consistently more likely to stress that a potentially cooperative and non-antagonistic relationship between unions and management was desirable. On one view, these data might be taken to imply some reduction of the union role stemming from the introduction of schemes. But given the positive correlation between trade unionism and profit sharing in the firm noted in Volume 1, our conclusions are rather more complex. That is to say, whereas the introduction of schemes may well produce a greater identification with the company's goals (and this applies particularly to non-unionists in a company where unions are recognized), it is unlikely that union activities will be completely undermined by profit sharing. But it is, in our view, important for unions to modify to some extent traditional sets of attitudes and assumptions in firms with profit sharing if they are to continue to retain an appeal to both trade unionists and non-trade unionists alike in the companies concerned.

Chapter four

Organizational commitment and performance

As we have indicated, it may well be that the effects of profit sharing and share ownership are greater on attitudes than on behaviour. To be sure, positive attitudes can, in turn, impact on practices in the company; but other factors (including those in the external environment of the firm) may well have a particularly pervasive impact on financial and industrial relations performance. In this chapter, this argument is further explored by an assessment of the consequences of schemes for organizational commitment and performance. Because of the importance attached to employee participation generally, we begin by examining the development of schemes in relation to involvement in decision-making in the company. This is followed by an assessment of the impact of schemes on organizational change and an examination of a wide range of employee attitudes themselves.

In Volume 1, we observed that the development of all-employee profit sharing and share ownership (and particularly SAYE schemes) is intimately connected with employee involvement in the company. Firms in which managements have adopted a consultative approach to industrial relations are particularly likely to have schemes and this relationship extends to employee involvement in actual decision-making on industrial relations issues and to the existence of union and non-union channels for employee participation. An important aspect of the case study phase was thus to assess the issue of employee participation in more detail. Indeed, in view of the centrality of this theme it was considered worthwhile to examine employee views on employee participation more generally, prior to a more specific review of their relationship to the presence of various schemes for profit sharing and share ownership.

Employee involvement

In the employee attitudes questionnaire we endeavoured to obtain information on the extent of involvement in decisions on the overall policies of the firm, in matters affecting both respondents' own departments and how jobs are done. Each of these areas of participation was examined under four main headings: (1) how much say or influence did employees in general in the firm *actually* have over decisions; (2) how much say or influence should employees in general have over decisions; (3) how much say or influence had the respondent actually has over decisions; and (4) how much say or influence should the respondent have over decisions.

The results are set out in Table 4.1. So far as employees actual say is concerned, respondents generally contrasted the situation with respect to the overall policies of the firm (where there was little perceived involvement) with how jobs were actually done (where the majority indicated that there was either some say or a great deal to say). For the desirable level of employee participation, a rather different pattern emerged. Indeed, in every instance (including the overall policies of the firm as well as departmental and job level decision-making) respondents indicated that they would like to see at least some employee say or influence over decision-making.

This pattern of results was paralleled by the data on the individual respondents' actual say over decision-making. As Table 4.1 again indicates, the majority of respondents felt that although they themselves had very little influence on the overall policies of the firm, they did have a far higher degree of involvement in how their jobs were actually performed. Interestingly, too, the majority of respondents appeared to desire some *personal* influence over the overall policies of the firm and, less surprisingly, a substantial involvement in task-based decision-making.

These data thus reveal considerable interest amongst respondents in employee participation in general. At job level there is clearly widespread participation in decisions but this would appear seldom to extend to policy levels. However, at the levels of the job, the department and the firm, respondents typically wished to see not only greater employee involvement but also to be themselves active participants in this process.

In order to assess both the strength and significance of these items and their links with views on profit sharing and share ownership, factor analysis was deployed and four factors were isolated. Table 4.2 shows employees' perception of actual and desired participation both collectively and individually at a number of organizational levels. The four underlying dimensions may be

Table 4.1 Employees' assessments of amount of say or influence there is in various situations

	No say at all 1	Very little say 2	Little say 3	Some say 4	Good deal of say 5	Great deal of say 6	Very great deal of say 7	Other	Mean (on 7 point scale)	SD
Employees' actual say										
1 Overall policies of firm	42	30	15	10	1	0	0	1	2.0	1.1
2 Matters affecting own department	8	26	16	36	10	2	1	1	3.2	1.3
3 How own jobs are done	5	11	12	42	22	6	1	1	3.9	1.3
Employees' desirable say										
1 Overall policies of firm	6	8	11	56	14	3	1	2	3.8	1.3
2 Matters affecting own department	1	1	3	32	41	15	6	2	4.8	1.0
3 How own jobs are done	0	1	2	21	37	23	14	2	5.2	1.1
Say individual respondent has										
1 Overall policies of firm	57	19	12	8	2	1	0	2	1.8	1.1
2 Matters affecting own department	13	19	15	27	13	7	3	2.1	3.4	1.6
3 How own job is done	4	10	11	32	22	12	7	2	4.3	1.5
Say individual respondent feels should exist										
1 Overall policies of firm	10	11	18	47	10	2	1	2	5.0	1.2
2 Matters affecting own department	2	2	4	33	33	15	8	2	4.8	1.2
3 How own job is done	1	1	2	19	32	24	19	2	5.3	1.2

Note: Percentages, n = 1931.

Table 4.2 Attitudes towards employee participation and views on profit-sharing and share-ownership schemes

	Profit sharing (cash)	Profit sharing (shares)	SAYE	Executive	Factor loading
Factor 1 – Desired participation					
Say or influence employees should have					
5 Matters affecting their own department	.05	−.02	−.01	−.05	0.84
6 How their own jobs are done	.04		.03	−.04	0.91
Say or influence respondent should have					
12 How respondent's own job is done	.05	.09**	.09**	.03	0.64
Factor 2 – Actual individual participation					
Respondent's actual say or influence					
8 Matters affecting their own department	−0.1	.18**	.12**	.22**	0.77
9 How their own jobs are done		.14**	.13**	.16**	0.81
Say or influence respondent should have					
11 Matters affecting respondent's own department	.06	.12**	.09**	.10**	0.68
Factor 3 – Actual collective participation					
Employees' actual say or influence					
1 Overall policies of firm	−.09**	.03	.03	.1**	0.63
2 Matters affecting their own department	−.03	.09**	.07*	.15**	0.86
3 How their own jobs are done	−.07*	.08**	.09**	.11**	0.79
Factor 4 – Participation in company policy					
Say or influence employees should have					
4 Overall policies of firm	−.03	−.06	−.02	−.05	0.76
Respondent's actual say or influence					
7 Overall policies of firm	−.02	.07*	.08*	.16**	0.60
Say or influence employees should have					
10 Overall policies of firm	.01	.01	.02	.03	0.79

Notes: Pearson product moment correlation coefficients – two-tailed significance.
  * Significant at 0.01 level.
  ** Significant at 0.001 level.
  The four factors account for 77.8 per cent of the shared variance.

referred to respectively as: (1) desired participation; (2) actual individual participation; (3) actual collective participation; and (4) participation in company policy.

Generally, the most significant relationships were found to be linked with views on share-based schemes. Moreover, the relationships were strongest for actual individual and collective participation and weakest for desired participation and participation in company policy making. This would suggest that favourable employee attitudes to share-ownership schemes are interconnected with the actual existence of participative machinery in the firm.

More specifically, as is indicated in Table 4.2, desired participation in how employees' own jobs are done, both collectively and individually, showed few significant relationships with attitudes to profit-sharing and share-ownership schemes. But it will be seen that a highly significant relationship was found between profit sharing with shares and SAYE-type schemes and desired individual participation at the lowest organizational level. This may well indicate that the more general share-based schemes increase the desire for direct individual participation, while the more selective share schemes do not.

In the second scale, as with the first, no significant relationships can be reported so far as the extent of participation and views on cash-based schemes are concerned. However, highly significant relationships were found between views on share-ownership schemes and actual participation at job and departmental levels. Weaker correlations were again found for SAYE-type schemes. This suggests that existing participative arrangements at these levels are again conducive to favourable attitudes to the more general share-based schemes.

In the third scale, highly significant relationships were found between actual collective participation at all organizational levels and views on executive share options (see again Table 4.2). Significant relationships were also found between views on profit sharing with shares and SAYE schemes and actual collective participation at departmental and job levels. However, a negative association was found between respondents' assessments of cash-based profit-sharing schemes and actual collective participation.

In the fourth scale, no significant relationships were found between the attitudes to schemes and desired collective and individual participation in the overall policies of the firm but a significant relationship was found between actual individual participation at this level and views on all share-ownership schemes. As is to be expected, there was a highly significant relationship between attitudes to executive share option schemes and respondents' actual say or influence in the overall policies of the company. This would suggest that a favourable attitude to share-based schemes is linked with the employee's perception of his or her individual say or influence at policy making levels.

We also sought to establish how far attitudes to employee participation are linked with actual ownership of sh res in the company. The relevant data we set out in Table 4.3, where some very interesting findings are observable. As is to be expected, employee shareholders have a greater say in how their jobs are

Table 4.3 Attitudes towards employee participation and company share ownership

	Shareholders N = 953		Non-shareholders N = 811		
	Mean	*SD*	*Mean*	*SD*	*t*
Employees' actual say or influence					
1 Overall policies of firm	2.0	1.1	2.0	1.1	− 1.24
2 Matters affecting their own department	3.2	1.3	3.2	1.2	0.0
3 How their own jobs are done	4.0	1.3	3.8	1.2	3.17**
Say or influence employees should have					
4 Overall policies of firm	3.8	1.1	3.8	1.2	− 0.76
5 Matters affecting their own department	4.8	1.0	4.8	1.1	− 0.80
6 How their own jobs are done	5.3	1.1	5.2	1.1	1.69*
Respondent's actual say or influence					
7 Overall policies of firm	1.8	1.2	1.7	1.1	2.27*
8 Matters affecting own department	3.6	1.6	3.3	1.5	4.01***
9 How own jobs are done	4.4	1.5	4.1	1.5	5.37***
Say or influence respondent should have					
10 Overall policies of firm	3.5	1.2	3.4	1.3	1.76*
11 Matters affecting respondent's own department	4.9	1.2	4.7	1.2	3.04**
12 How respondent's own job is done	5.5	1.1	5.2	1.2	4.43***

Notes: * = p 0.10, two-tailed.
         ** = p 0.05, two-tailed.
        *** = p 0.01, two-tailed.
       **** = p 0.001, two-tailed.

done. Moreover, the differences are particularly pronounced so far as the individual respondent's actual influence is concerned. But what is especially noticeable is that share ownership is strongly linked with a desire for greater personal influence over decision-making (and this applies to the overall policies of the firm, as well as to matters affecting one's own department and how the respondent's actual job is done). In short, employees who participate in share schemes in the company are likely to want personally to participate in decision-making processes as well. And this of course reinforces a recurrent theme of this research project, that the various types of employee involvement (financial and decision-making) are interconnected.

Organizational change

Data from the employee attitudes survey thus revealed some interesting linkages between views on profit-sharing and share-ownership schemes and participation in decision-making within the firm. But participation in decisions and employee financial involvement have been widely advocated as means of achieving greater organizational flexibility and commitment in an increasingly competitive economic environment. Key respondents were thus asked to what extent the introduction of profit-sharing and share-ownership schemes had contributed to the acceptance of organizational change.

In at least one case study company, it was found that a dramatic organizational change had been made smoother as a result of employee involvement practices in general, of which profit sharing and share ownership were a part. But the most interesting finding was that organizational change was often a stimulus for profit sharing and share ownership. This was manifested in three ways: (1) privatization; (2) merger and takeover; and (3) the movement towards more competitive market oriented strategies and the consequences for organizational structure that this entailed. Indeed, it is obvious that privatization has important consequences for the potential development of employee share ownership, not least when employees are the receivers of shares accompanying a change in ownership. Moreover, merger and takeover can have substantial implications for employees if policy in these respects alters alongside a major reshaping of the structure of the constituent organization.

Furthermore, the case of a retail firm provided an indication of the implications of a change in management policy towards competitiveness and the growth of share-ownership schemes. This company witnessed a major improvement in profits between 1982 and 1985 (an increase of 138 per cent), accompanying a major reduction in the workforce (cut by half between 1980 and 1986). During this period, the original family owner lost control (though it still retained 45 per cent of share capital). The nature of the firm also changed and with it there was a move to a competitive market oriented policy of which profit sharing and share ownership were a part. In short, employee financial participation in this firm did not specifically facilitate organizational change, but part of the impetus for initiating share-ownership schemes arose from the major transformation in company policy and structure which took place in the 1980s.

Employee attitudes

But to what extent, it may be reasonably asked, does profit sharing and share ownership impact upon attitudes to the employing organization? This central issue is now addressed in more detail, using data from the employee attitudes survey. We begin this analysis by an examination of the effects of ownership on attitudes to various types of schemes. This is followed by an account of perceived effects of schemes on various aspects of organizational performance.

Share ownership

There is no doubt first of all that ownership of shares in the company (and in other companies) is strongly associated with positive attitudes towards profit sharing and share ownership. The direction of this linkage is difficult to determine, and there are, in any case, likely to be interactive relationships. Correlation analysis was used to examine the relationship between employee attitudes to profit-sharing and share-ownership schemes and their ownership of shares in the employing company and in any other company. As is shown in Table 4.4, highly significant relationships were found between views on share-based profit-sharing and SAYE schemes both in terms of ownership of shares in the employing company and in other companies.

These findings are amplified in Table 4.5, which reveals the differences between owners and non-owners of shares based on the mean scores of each group of respondents. It will be seen that there are highly significant differences in attitudes to both profit-sharing (share-based) and SAYE schemes depending on ownership or non-ownership of share in the company.

Table 4.4 Ownership of shares and views of employees on profit sharing or share ownership

	Profit sharing (cash)	Profit sharing (shares)	SAYE	Executive
Owns share in company	− .07*	.17**	.19**	.05
Owns shares in other companies	.02	.15**	.15**	.14**

Notes: Pearson product moment correlation coefficients – two-tailed significance.
   * Significant at 0.01 level.
  ** Significant at 0.001 level.

Table 4.5 Employee attitudes to profit-sharing and share-ownership schemes by company share ownership

	Shareholders N = 746		Non-shareholders N = 717		
	Mean	SD	Mean	SD	t
Profit sharing (cash)	1.69	0.78	1.60	0.68	2.34**
Profit sharing (shares)	1.78	0.89	2.06	0.88	− 6.03****
SAYE	2.10	0.95	2.38	0.88	− 5.98****
Executive	2.89	1.20	3.01	0.95	− 2.08**

Notes: * = p 0.10, two-tailed.
    ** = p 0.05, two-tailed.
   *** = p 0.01, two-tailed.
  **** = p 0.001, two-tailed.

Impact on work practices

The introduction of share-based profit-sharing schemes in the company thus almost certainly impacts upon employee attitudes to profit sharing. But in many respects a more important issue is the impact on work practices. Respondents were asked to assess (on a seven point scale) to what extent the introduction of schemes had affected: (1) satisfaction and job security; (2) work effort; and (3) employee involvement and communications. As can be seen from Table 4.6, the majority of respondents detected little change in these respects, though satisfaction in working for the given concern was a marked exception. Nevertheless, there was generally a balance of positive over negative responses on such issues as communications between management and worker, effort put into work, the amount of productive work done and the amount of effort other people put into their jobs. Clearly, then, profit sharing and share ownership had few negative consequences and may well have affected a series of worthwhile but modest improvements in employees' attitudes and work performance.

Table 4.6 Employees' assessments of the effects of schemes on aspects of their work

Effects of introduction of schemes on	Decreased greatly			Not changed			Increased greatly	Other	Mean	SD
	1	2	3	4	5	6	7			
1 Overall satisfaction in working for firm	1	2	4	48	28	12	3	3	4.5	1.0
2 Feeling of job security	1	2	6	72	11	5	1	3	4.1	0.8
3 Effort put into work	0	0	1	67	17	8	4	3	4.4	0.8
4 Amount of productive work done	0	0	1	68	16	8	3	3	4.4	0.8
5 Amount of effort other people put into jobs	0	1	3	68	18	5	1	3	4.3	0.7
6 Employees' say concerning jobs	1	3	5	74	11	2	0	3	4.3	0.7
7 Employees' say in departments	2	3	5	75	11	2	0	3	4.0	0.7
8 Employees' say in overall policies of firm	2	3	5	73	10	3	1	4	4.0	0.8
9 Your say in decisions concerning job	2	2	4	75	11	2	1	3	4.0	0.8
10 Your say in decisions concerning department	2	2	4	76	10	3	1	3	4.0	0.8
11 Your say in decisions concerning overall policies of firm	2	2	3	84	5	0	0	3	3.9	0.6
12 Communication between management and workers	3	5	5	57	22	4	1	3	4.1	1.0

Note: Percentages, n = 1931.

Further analysis was undertaken by means of factor analysis to assess the relative strengths and significance of these items with views on profit-sharing and share-ownership schemes. As will be seen in Table 4.7, two factors were isolated and referred respectively to: (1) involvement in the company; and (2) increased productivity. It will be seen that there are highly significant associations between employees' attitudes to all profit-sharing and share-ownership schemes and employees' overall satisfaction in working for the firm. Moreover, the strongest associations are clearly with share-based schemes. In general, then, positive employee attitudes to share-based schemes are consistent with employees' perceptions of improved satisfaction and security at work together with improved employee involvement, both collectively and individually, at all organizational levels.

With respect to improvements in productivity, generally the associations are not as strong but they are significant for share-based profit sharing. In particular, a perception of increased amount of effort put into the job and the amount of productive work done is linked with views on profit sharing schemes more generally. Views on share-based schemes thus do relate to increased employee involvement, satisfaction and security at work and a perception of increased effort and the amount of productive work done in the organization.

Furthermore, we sought to establish how far ownership of shares in the company is linked with attitudes to the impact of schemes. In general, there were few highly significant differences between owners and non-owners. However, employee shareholders were particularly likely to indicate that overall satisfaction in working for the firm had increased following the adoption of schemes by their companies (t = 4.89***).

Organizational identity

Respondents were also asked to indicate their views on a series of issues relating to company, work and career. Table 4.8 sets out employees' assessments of their sense of organizational identity and belongingness in the company. It will be seen that although a substantial number of respondents felt a sense of pride in working for their firms, at the same time, few had any real sense of ownership and most indicated that they 'simply felt like an employee'. Clearly, then, the introduction of profit sharing in the company has not broken down entrenched attitudes to work of this type.

Further analysis (Table 4.9) showed that views on share-based and executive share schemes were related to employees' attitudes to

Table 4.7 Employee attitudes to work and profit sharing or share ownership

	Profit sharing (cash)	Profit sharing (shares)	SAYE	Executive	Factor loading
Factor 1 – Involvement in the company					
1 Overall satisfaction in working for the firm	.09**	.3**	.2**	.2**	0.57
2 Feeling of job security	.04	.15**	.07**	.14**	0.60
3 Employees' say in decisions concerning their own jobs	.03	.1**	.05	.13**	0.85
4 Employees' say in decisions concerning their own departments	.03	.13**	.06	.17**	0.89
5 Employees' say in overall policies of the firm	.03	.15**	.08**	.18**	0.82
6 Respondents' say in decisions concerning their own jobs	.04	.11**	.08**	.18**	0.82
7 Respondents' say in decisions in their own departments	.03	.12**	.09**	.17**	0.78
8 Respondents' say in overall policies of the firm	.03	.12**	.08**	.17**	0.79
9 Communication between managers and workers	.05	.17**	.12**	.22**	0.73
Factor 2 – Increased productivity					
1 Amount of effort put into job	.07*	.09**		.02	0.85
2 Amount of productive work	.07*	.08**	.03	.01	0.89
3 Amount of effort other people at work put into their jobs	.04	.07*	.03	.08**	0.70

Notes: Pearson product moment correlation coefficients – two-tailed significance.
* Significant at 0.01 level.
** Significant at 0.001 level.
The two factors account for 62.8 per cent of the shared variance.

Table 4.8 Employees' assessments on sense of belongingness in company

	Little extent						Very great extent	Other	Mean	SD
	1	2	3	4	5	6	7			
1 Feel a sense of ownership	38	25	15	13	5	2	1	3	2.3	1.4
2 Simply feel like an employee	9	9	10	18	12	14	26	3	4.7	2.0
3 Feel a sense of self employment	50	14	12	12	5	2	1	4	2.1	1.5
4 Feel a sense of pride in working here	7	6	9	27	25	13	11	3	4.4	1.6

Note: Percentages, n = 1931.

Table 4.9 Belongingness and attitudes to profit sharing or share ownership

	Profit sharing (cash)	Profit sharing (shares)	SAYE	Executive
1 Feel a sense of ownership	.02	.17**	.16**	.18**
2 Simply feel like an employee	−.03	−.11**	−.06***	−.1**
3 Feel a sense of self employment		.07**	.01	.12**
4 Feel a sense of pride working here		.18**	.11**	.16**

Notes: Pearson product moment correlation coefficients – two-tailed significance.

  ** Significant at 0.001 level.

their status in the company. Clearly, profit-sharing and share-ownership schemes have not fundamentally altered certain basic sets of attitudes and produced personnel who no longer consider themselves to have the status of employees. However, views on schemes are related to broader attitudes on organizational identity and the extent to which employees' experience a sense of ownership, self employment and pride in working for the company.

Work and career

We were concerned to discover whether the introduction of profit-sharing and shareholding schemes in the company impacted on attitudes to work and career. Table 4.10 sets out employees' views on these issues. It will be seen that there was less of an instrumental approach to work than probably exists in companies without schemes. After all, less than half of our respondents agreed or strongly agreed with the view that 'the most important element in any job is the pay'. Moreover, a substantial majority (72 per cent) considered it to be important for an employee to feel part of the company.

The majority of respondents, however, did consider that work and home should be sharply separated. Given the earlier data on participation, there was perhaps less support for the view that 'it is essential for the employee to participate in decision-making' than might have been expected. There was in general a rejection of the statement that 'the best representative of the employee's interest is the union not the company'. The considerable importance attached to 'high trust' relationships between management and the workforce is particularly noteworthy (two-thirds of respondents strongly agreeing with the statement that 'it is important for management and the workforce to trust one another'). Finally, there was probably a higher level of company rather than individual career commitment than might have been expected. Indeed, only a minority of respondents agreed or strongly agreed with the view that 'a person's own individual career is more important than any loyalty to a particular company'.

Of course it is difficult to know whether or not these attitudes would also be held by employees in companies without profit-sharing or shareholding schemes. But these data lend support to the view that employee attitudes are affected by financial participation and, in particular, that commitment to the company develops as a consequence.

And yet orientations to work and career are not strongly linked with views on profit-sharing schemes. Based on factor analysis, the

Table 4.10 Employees' views on statements regarding work and career

| | Strongly agree | | | | Strongly disagree | | | |
	1	2	3	4	5	Other	Mean	SD
1 The most important element in any job is the pay	18	23	34	13	10	3	2.7	1.2
2 It is important for an employee to feel fully a part of the company	34	38	20	3	2	2	2.0	0.9
3 It is essential for the employee to participate in decision-making	17	31	36	11	3	3	2.5	1.0
4 Work and home should be sharply separated	39	21	23	10	5	3	2.2	1.2
5 The best representative of the employees' interests in the union not the company	6	9	19	11	11	44*	3.1	1.3
6 It is important for management and the workforce to trust one another	66	22	5	2	2	2	1.5	0.9
7 A person's own individual career is more important than any loyalty to a particular company	16	22	33	15	11	3	2.8	1.2

Notes: Percentages, n = 1931.
* A substantial number of respondents did not answer this specific question.

relevant data are set out in Table 4.11. It will be seen that views on share-based profit sharing are again most closely linked with other sets of attitudes. Two factors referring to trust and instrumental relations respectively were isolated and a positive commitment to share-based schemes was found to be associated with: (1) an emphasis on the employee feeling fully a part of the company; and (2) relationships of trust between management and the workforce. Moreover, such attitudes were linked with a rejection of the view that the most important element in any job is the pay and the importance of individual career over loyalty to the company. Hence, while the relationship between views on profit sharing and trust and instrumental relations in the firm are in the expected direction, they are not substantial enough to support the argument that attitudes to work and career can be radically transformed by the adoption of profit-sharing and share-ownership schemes.

Interrelationships between attitudes

In order to trace the links between employee attitudes and views on profit sharing in more detail, it is worth examining the underlying pattern of relationships between the composite variables identified by factor analysis. In Table 4.12, the results are set out based on four groups of composite variables. These are: (1) individual participation and organizational identity; (2) economic rewards (see also Table 2.6); (3) productivity; and (4) trust.

Factor analysis of the composite variables shows that the strongest and most significant association is between employee attitudes to profit-sharing and share-ownership schemes and what we have termed economic rewards. These, it will be recalled, relate to the views of employees on how far various financial objectives of management in introducing schemes have been met in practice (see Chapter 2). This suggests that the perception of the financial success of schemes is particularly central to a positive assessment of profit-sharing and share-ownership schemes.

Weaker but highly significant associations were found between views on schemes, and individual and collective participation and organizational identity. Certainly, the existence of individual and collective means of participation favours a positive attitude to profit-sharing and share-ownership schemes in general and this participation is reinforced by an organizational identity among the employees. Relationships of similar strength and significance were also found in relation to increased employee involvement and productivity. This, as we have seen, indicates that a favourable attitude to profit-sharing and share-ownership schemes encourages

Table 4.11 Orientations to work and profit sharing or share ownership

	Profit sharing (cash)	Profit sharing (shares)	SAYE	Executive	Factor loadings
Factor 1 – Trust relations					
1 Important for an employee to feel fully a part of the company	.07*	.11*	.07*	– .04	0.81
2 Essential for the employee to participate in decision-making	.05	– .01	– .02	– .11**	0.64
3 Important for management and the workforce to trust one another	.05	.10**	.06	.04	0.69
Factor 2 – Instrumental relations					
4 The most important element in any job is the pay	.07*	– .07*	– .05	– .11**	0.69
5 Work and home should be sharply separated	.06*	– .06	– .03	– .03	0.53
6 A person's own individual career is more important than any loyalty to a particular company	.01	– .09**	– .03	– .06	0.72

Notes: Pearson product moment correlation coefficients – two-tailed significance.
  * Significant at 0.01 level.
  ** Significant at 0.001 level.
  The two factors account for 50.0 per cent of the shared variance.

Table 4.12 Factor analysis of composite variables and profit sharing and share ownership

	All schemes	Profit sharing (cash)	Profit sharing (shares)	SAYE	Executive	Factor loadings
Factor 1 – Individual participation and organizational identity						
Desired participation	.03	.05	.03	.04	.02	0.54
Actual individual participation	.21**	.02	.18**	.14**	.20**	0.80
Actual collective participation	.10**	−.07*	.09**	.08**	.15**	0.69
Participation in company policy	.07	.01	.01	.03	.06	0.69
Ownership identity	.18**	−.02	.18**	.13**	.20**	0.55
Factor 2 – Economic rewards						
Financial incentives	.30**	.09*	.28**	.22**	.25**	0.69
Financial rewards	.33**	.09**	.33**	.28**	.24**	0.77
Factor 3 – Productivity						
Involvement in the company	.27**	.07*	.23**	.15**	.25**	0.82
Increased productivity	.10**	.06	.11**	.05	.10**	0.84
Factor 4 – Trust						
Trust relations	−.05	−.09**	−.05	−.02	.03	0.79
Instrumental relations	.10**	−.05	.11**	.05	.10**	0.55

Notes: Pearson product moment correlation coefficients – two-tailed significance.
    * Significant at 0.01 level.
    ** Significant at 0.001 level.
    The four factors account for 60.4 per cent of the shared variance.

improved satisfaction, security and the perceived need for increased employee involvement in work (particularly in the form of increased communication between management and workforce). Moreover, although the links are weaker in the case of productivity, a positive attitude of profit-sharing and share-ownership schemes does indicate a positive view on the effects of the introduction of schemes on productive effort.

Conclusions

In sum, our data suggest that there is a complex and interdependent set of employees' attitudes, of which views on profit sharing and share ownership are an integral component. There is no doubt that employee attitudes in the company are affected by employee financial participation. And positive views on schemes are certainly associated with a wide range of further favourable attitudes to the financial and productive performance of the firms, employee participation and a perceived cooperative atmosphere between management and the workforce. Hence, notwithstanding the limitations to the effects of profit sharing and share ownership on behaviour in the company (arising not least from the impact of wider environmental forces), the argument that employee financial participation is linked with a positive set of attitudes on a wide range of aspects of company policy clearly received considerable support from this inquiry.

Chapter five

Detailed case study analysis of the impact of schemes

One of the most important findings of this investigation is that profit sharing and share ownership are a highly complex phenomenon and that simple causal notions of the origins and impact of schemes do not reflect realities within companies. In the first volume, we were able to show that the genesis of employee financial participation stems from managerial strategic choices. But we also found that these are set within a wide range of environmental and organizational conditions which are conducive to the emergence of given practices. In this second volume, we have observed that the consequences of profit sharing and share ownership are very difficult to disentangle from other forces which may be of greater influence on actual outcomes. Moreover, even if it is reasonable to argue that schemes have a more direct and pronounced impress upon attitudes than upon behaviour, it is still necessary to understand that this process is itself interactive and that a mutually reinforcing set of attitudes is readily identifiable in practice.

The case study stage of the research offered a unique opportunity to examine in more detail these interrelated patterns. Indeed, three main sets of data are available for analysis purposes. These comprise: (1) the views of key respondents on the objectives involved in setting up schemes and on a variety of issues associated with their actual operation; (2) time series data on the background financial circumstances when particular schemes in given firms were introduced, coupled with the material on economic and industrial relations performance; and (3) the views of employees, not only on profit sharing and share ownership in general, but also on whether the introduction of schemes has had any marked effect upon their work performance and attitudes.

Indeed, the linkage of the various sets of data in a number of cases reveals a most interesting interrelationship between managerial objectives, the financial experiences of companies and employee views. In this chapter, then, three contrasting companies are examined in this rather different way. In each company, the objectives of managers in introducing schemes are first set out, followed by an examination of the financial profiles of firms and an outline and discussion of the views of the employees themselves.

Case 1: A finance sector company

The first case to be examined is a leading bank in Britain. In 1985, it employed 66,243 employees, though its workforce had been slowly declining from a total of 71,800 employees in 1981. The company was one of the first to take advantage of profit-sharing and share-ownership legislation and, indeed, its APS scheme was introduced in 1979. It also had two SAYE schemes. The first (A scheme) had been established in 1979 (and enjoyed no concessions on income tax), while the second (B scheme) had been adopted in 1981 under the 1980 Act provisions. There were also two Executive Share Option (ESO) schemes; the A scheme being yet again set up in 1979, with the B scheme coming into effect in 1985 under the 1984 Act provisions.

The managerial objectives in introducing these various schemes differed somewhat depending on: (a) the diverse aims of managers in different functions; and (b) the types of scheme. The schemes originally emerged from a distinctive industrial relations policy and they were seen to form a significant benefit in terms of an overall 'remuneration package' which the firm was developing. Currently, however, control of the schemes is under the aegis of the Administration/Compensation Department and not the Industrial Relations Department and this would appear to have had implications for the different types of objectives which are now encompassed.

The original pressure from the Industrial Relations Department to establish schemes was thus clearly manifested in the types of scheme adopted and their objectives. To begin with, then, the introduction of both the A schemes was conceived in terms of a comprehensive reward and remuneration package for employees. In 1979, only the APS scheme enjoyed full tax concessions, but both the SAYE and ESO schemes were adopted in that year since they were deemed to be valuable as a means of extending the range of remuneration options for the company. It is also significant that such origins were associated with the early introduction of the schemes.

However, the transfer of responsibilities for the schemes to the more 'finance' oriented Administration/Compensation Department was accompanied by a change in objectives perceived for the schemes themselves even though these did not appear to have been directly communicated to the employees. Indeed, in 1989, two main objectives were viewed as uppermost: (1) to remain competitive within the finance sector, where similar types of benefit for employees were being provided; and (2) to change employee attitudes so that they understood the make up of the company and the usefulness of share capital. Moreover, both A schemes were phased out, in 1981 and 1985, because they were seen as unnecessary, given the changes in legislation, and the subsequent B schemes that the company had introduced.

This particular company was a valuable example of the different (but not necessarily competing) objectives of managers in the main functional specialisms of the firm with respect to profit sharing and share ownership. It also, as we shall see, highlighted well the relationship between a favourable financial performance and the introduction of schemes, and the way in which adverse circumstances can influence profitability irrespective of whether or not profit-sharing or employee share-ownership schemes have been introduced.

Turning to the relationship between financial performance and the introduction of profit sharing and share ownership in the company, Table 5.1 sets out the data on profits before and after tax, earnings per share and net ordinary dividend per share, for the years 1976–85 inclusive. It is striking that in the key year of 1979 when APS, SAYE and ESO schemes were all adopted, pre- and post-tax profits were at a peak and that earnings per £1 share were higher than in any subsequent year. The stimulus provided by profitability for the introduction of schemes is thus once again reinforced. It is also particularly interesting that profits plummeted in 1984 because of the collapse of a foreign subsidiary bank, an exigency which was to occasion a fall in the share price internationally. Indeed management freely admitted that this dramatic circumstance had overridden any endeavours of employees themselves to improve productivity and profitability.

The firm recognized two unions (BIFU and ASTMS) and was about 50 per cent unionized. It had both collective bargaining and consultative arrangements for involving employees, although neither directly impacted upon the schemes. However, advance notice of the introduction of schemes was given to the unions and they were also consulted as the schemes developed. Full-time officials in both unions were contacted by the research team and the general view was that, although the unions had no overall policy on profit sharing and share ownership, they were not opposed to these developments so long as they did not impinge on

collective bargaining. However, the officials would have liked to
see the schemes negotiable in terms of both of their establishment
and subsequent operation. Employees were informed directly
about the schemes by means of a booklet and covering letter in a
folder.

Table 5.1 A finance sector company: profits before and after tax,
earnings and net ordinary dividend per share

Year	Profits before tax £m	Profit/loss after tax £m	Earnings per £1 share p	Net ordinary dividend per £1 share p
1976	167	99	71.3	12.48
1977	197	112	81.3	14.58
1978	231	143	88.8	16.44
1979	315	192	117.4	20.00
1980	230	168	102.7	21.35
1981	231	192	109.0	24.0
1982	251	170	82.4	25.5
1983	225	125	60.6	25.5
1984	135	− 25	27.1	25.5
1985	351	144	53.0	25.5

The employees' attitudes to profit-sharing and share-ownership
schemes in general were, for the most part, highly favourable.
Indeed 95 per cent of employers were either in favour or strongly in
favour of profit sharing through cash awards, 78 per cent
supported profit sharing through shares in the company and 61 per
cent endorsed SAYE schemes. There was also a balance of positive
over negative views on the ESO schemes, though consistent with
the pattern in other firms, the largest single group (49 per cent of
respondents) were neither in favour nor against these types of
arrangement.

However, given the adverse circumstances experienced by the
firm occasioned by the collapse of the overseas subsidiary, it was
particularly interesting to examine the levels of satisfaction of
employees with the rewards of their particular company's schemes.
Table 5.2 sets out the relevant information and it will be seen that,
for the most part, employees were satisfied with their own company's schemes in this respect. However, few employees were
highly satisfied and, a sizeable minority (23 per cent) considered
that the rewards from the APS scheme were unsatisfactory (this is
scarcely surprising in view of the uneven profits performance of the
firm, which had little to do with the behaviour of the workforce).
Employees in this firm, too, had a particularly marked preference

Table 5.2 Degree of satisfaction of employees with the rewards of profit sharing and share ownership from the finance sector company's particular scheme

Type of scheme	Highly satisfactory	Satisfactory	Neither satisfactory nor unsatisfactory	Unsatisfactory	Highly unsatisfactory	Other/ don't know/ no response	Mean	SD
Profit sharing (APS)	2	51	17	23	6	1	2.8	1.0
Share ownership (SAYE)	4	45	33	10	3	5	2.6	0.8
Executive share option (ESO)	1	16	54	8	3	18	2.9	0.7

Note: Percentages, n = 279.

for *cash*-based entitlements (53 per cent preferring this method of allocation) and this is again not surprising given the dramatic alterations in the profitability of the firm over time and in earnings per share. It is also instructive that only 26 per cent of respondents participated in their firm's SAYE scheme.

Moreover, some particularly interesting findings emerged from the employees' attitudes in this firm with respect to their assessments of the effects of schemes and on whether or not various managerial objectives had been fulfilled. The relevant data are set out in Tables 5.3 and 5.4 and, although, the overall pattern of responses is not markedly dissimilar from that of the sample as a whole, there is a clear tendency for this company's employees: (a) to emphasize the improvements in satisfaction, productive effort, employee involvement, and communications; but (b) to be especially likely to indicate that the schemes had been unsuccessful in achieving various managerial objectives.

In Table 5.3, then, although the majority of employees sampled in the firm indicated that few changes had stemmed from the introduction of schemes, the marginal improvements detected by substantial minorities of respondents in the respects of overall satisfaction in working for the firm, effort put into work, productive work done, amount of effort people put into their jobs and in communication between management and workers are worth noting. But of special interest is to contrast these perceptions with views on how far various managerial objectives had been fulfilled (see Table 5.4). Indeed, clear majorities of respondents indicated that, in their view, the company's schemes had been unsuccessful or not at all successful in making employees more profit conscious, in acting as an incentive to greater productivity, in providing a tax efficient means of reward for employees and the company and in ensuring that employees benefited from the company's profitability. Moreover, in each case, these percentages are higher than those applying for the overall sample of employees in the survey. And, although there may of course be several reasons for these differences, it is likely that part of the explanation lies in the adverse profits performance of the firm in 1984 which must surely have led to several employees doubting the advantages of their company's schemes in terms of objectives associated with profitability and rewards. Furthermore, these data reinforce the view that employees' attitudes towards their firm's schemes may become less favourable in adverse financial circumstances even if the workforce remains broadly committed to profit sharing and share ownership as a general principle.

In sum, this financial sector company is a particularly interesting

Table 5.3 A finance sector company: employees' assessments of the effects of schemes on aspects of their work

Effects of introduction of schemes on	Decreased greatly			Not changed			Increased greatly	Other	Mean	SD
	1	2	3	4	5	6	7			
1 Overall satisfaction in working for firm	0	1	3	45	37	11	1	1	4.6	0.9
2 Feeling of job security	1	1	6	79	10	3	0	1	4.0	0.7
3 Effort put into work	0	0	0	60	25	9	4	1	4.6	0.8
4 Amount of productive work done	0	0	1	60	27	8	3	1	4.5	0.8
5 Amount of effort other people put into jobs	0	1	2	61	27	7	1	1	4.4	0.7
6 Employees' say concerning jobs	0	5	2	76	14	3	1	1	4.1	0.7
7 Employees' say in departments	2	2	3	74	15	4	0	2	4.2	0.6
8 Employees' say in overall policies of firm	2	1	3	71	16	5	0	2	4.2	0.8
9 Your say in decisions concerning job	1	2	3	74	17	2	0	1	4.1	0.6
10 Your say in decisions concerning department	0	2	3	76	14	3	0	1	4.1	0.6
11 Your say in decisions concerning overall policies of firm	2	2	4	83	7	1	0	1	4.0	0.6
12 Communication between management and workers	1	3	5	48	34	7	0	1	4.3	0.9

Note: Percentages, n = 279. Consistent with the questionnaire item, the scales run from negative to positive.

Table 5.4 A finance sector company: employees' estimates of the success of schemes in terms of a number of objectives

Objectives	Very successful 1	Successful 2	Neither successful nor unsuccessful 3	Unsuccessful 4	Not at all successful 5	Don't know	No response	Mean	SD
1 To make employees more profit conscious/more interested in the company's success	1	4	23	61	8	2	1	3.8	1.0
2 To increase employees' sense of commitment to the company/ make staff more liable to stay	3	11	50	31	3	2	1	3.3	1.1
3 Act as incentive to greater productivity	1	7	33	51	4	1	2	3.6	0.9
4 To make employees feel that they are part of a company – working *with* it, not just for it	7	9	39	39	4	2	1	3.3	1.2
5 To help to hold down wage claims	6	20	51	11	5	6	1	3.3	1.7
6 To provide a tax efficient means of reward for employees	2	6	33	45	7	5	2	3.8	1.5
for company	0	2	32	40	11	12	3	4.3	1.9
7 To ensure that employees benefit from the company's profitability	1	4	22	54	6	3	1	3.7	0.8
8 To increase employees' understanding of the financial issues that face the company	4	9	50	30	1	4	2	3.4	1.4
9 To increase the sense of cooperation between management and workforce	6	11	55	23	2	1	3	3.1	1.0

Note: Percentages, n = 279.

case in illustrating at least four main points. In the first place, it reveals how managers in different departments variously view the objectives of schemes and how priorities can change when there is a shift in responsibility for the schemes from industrial relations to finance-type departments. Secondly, it reinforces the view that a highly favourable financial performance in a given year is not infrequently associated with the introduction of profit-sharing and share-ownership schemes. Thirdly, it shows how major events (such as a collapse of a foreign subsidiary) can impact far more on profitability than profit-sharing or employee share-ownership schemes. And fourthly, it reveals how employee views can be affected by such adverse circumstances and, that despite remaining overwhelmingly favourable to schemes in general, they may well consider that various managerial objectives in introducing schemes in their particular firms have, as a consequence, been far from fulfilled in actual practice.

Case 2: A manufacturing company

For the second case, a leading brewing group in the UK has been selected for analysis. It employed 21,866 full-time and 25,255 part-time employees in 1986, the former being particularly concentrated in the brewing units and the latter in the licensed premises. The company had introduced an APS scheme in 1980, a SAYE share option scheme in 1975, and an ESO scheme had been set up in 1971. There were modifications to the SAYE and ESO schemes in 1981 and 1985 respectively following legislation. Furthermore, in 1986, for senior managers in North America, an ESO scheme was established. This, however, did not enjoy tax concessions in the UK, a situation which ensured that key managers were seeking changes in legislation to alter this state of affairs.

By comparison with the financial sector company examined earlier, there appeared to be a greater consistency in the policy and objectives of managers when the schemes were actually being introduced. Indeed, the company secretary and group personnel director of the firm were both responsible for the schemes and the objectives underlying them were part of a coherent industrial relations strategy encompassed in a booklet provided to all employees and entitled the *'Brewco' Way* (which also outlined the general philosophy/culture of the company and its views on its employees). Hence, the main aim of the schemes was seen to be to give the employees a share in the long term prospects of the company. The schemes were not regarded as an immediate bonus but as a 'long term incentive'. Ownership was viewed as more important than remuneration. And the schemes, it was hoped, would increase interest in the fortunes of the company and result in positive employee attitudes and behaviour to their employing organization.

Compared with the finance sector company examined earlier in this chapter, there was an important and remarkably consistent improvement in profits, earnings and dividends per share and annual turnover over roughly the same ten year period. The relevant data are set out in Table 5.5, which traces the pattern on these indices for the years 1975–86 inclusive. It will be seen that, with the exception of a slight reduction in earnings per share in 1982 and 1983, in any given year the company's financial performance had improved from the previous one and that the typical pattern was of a steady rather than uneven advance.

So far as the timing of the introduction of schemes is concerned, there were no appreciable delays occasioned by an adverse profits performance. Moreover, the adoption of schemes was consistent with a progressive improvement in financial performance. But the development of schemes was related to an overall industrial relations policy and was part of a general aim to increase the employees' sense of well being and commitment to the company.

Table 5.5 A manufacturing company: profits before tax, earnings and net ordinary dividend per share and annual turnover

Year	Profits before tax £m	Earnings per share (25p)	Net ordinary dividend per share (25p)	Turnover £m
1975	20.8	6.2	2.0	331.0
1976	29.9	6.5	2.1	433.8
1977	41.9	9.2	2.4	508.5
1978	43.5	10.8	2.7	562.2
1979	54.4	13.0	3.2	645.2
1980	61.8	14.4	4.0	720.3
1981	66.4	15.1	4.5	782.1
1982	73.3	14.3	4.9	841.7
1983	81.0	14.1	5.4	1,001.9
1984	95.1	19.3	6.3	1,185.7
1985	110.1	21.4	7.0	1,444.0
1986	129.6	23.0	7.8	1,533.0

The unions recognized by the company included the TGWU, GMBATU, the National Association of Licensed House Managers and USDAW, though only the first two were of course represented in the actual manufacturing (brewing) plants. In the firm as a whole, between 50 and 55 per cent of full-time employees were unionized and there were local collective bargaining arrangements.

Procedural arrangements were negotiated in approximately 40–50 local units organized by geographical area and business sector. All bargaining units were largely independent of central control although both the share schemes and pension arrangements were organized on a national basis. The share schemes were not negotiable, though they were sometimes discussed in the consultative committees which had been established in the firm. The union officials in the TGWU and GMBATU took the view that, so long as the firm's schemes did not impinge upon collective bargaining they would be broadly supported. Employees were informed directly about the schemes through video, booklets and briefing sessions.

The employees surveyed were employed in a single manufacturing site in South Wales. The TGWU was the principle union and although there was no closed shop agreement in the plant, the bulk of manual workers (and over 50 per cent of the workforce as a whole) were union members.

The attitudes of the employees here were particularly interesting because the work site combined the circumstances of: (1) a well established workforce in a traditional industry, with (2) an uninterrupted and impressive financial performance of the wider company, enabling it to provide secure employment and consistent benefits in a region with unemployment above the UK national average. Moreover, as we shall see, these twin conditions appeared to be related to considerable support for profit sharing and share ownership in general and for the particular company's schemes. Indeed, the level of commitment of the employees to their *own* firm's arrangements was appreciably greater than in the case of the finance sector firm which we have just examined (see Tables 5.2 and 5.6), despite the different occupational and industrial sector characteristics of the two workforces. The importance of a firm making consistently good and, preferably rising, profits for a highly positive set of attitudes to a particular company's scheme thus appears to be underscored.

To begin with, employee attitudes towards profit sharing and share ownership in general were highly positive (over half of respondents in each case strongly in favour of profit sharing with cash awards, profit sharing through shares in the company and SAYE schemes, with hardly a respondent being negative in each case). The company's share-ownership (APS) and 'own as you earn' (SAYE) schemes were also typically supported in terms of the rewards actually accruing to employees (78 per cent of respondents considering the APS scheme to be either satisfactory or highly satisfactory and 70 per cent supporting the SAYE scheme in these

Table 5.6 Degree of satisfaction of employees with the rewards of profit sharing and share ownership from the manufacturing company's particular scheme

	Highly satisfactory				Highly unsatisfactory	Other/not applicable	Mean	SD
	1	2	3	4	5			
'Brewco' share-ownership (APS) scheme	17.3	60.6	15.4	5.8	1.0	0	2.1	0.8
'Brewco' own as you earn (SAYE) scheme	25.0	45.2	17.3	1.0	1.0	10.6	2.0	0.8

Note: Percentages, n = 104.

respects). Moreover, only 7 per cent of respondents felt that the APS scheme as unsatisfactory or highly unsatisfactory and only 2 per cent indicated negative attitudes to the SAYE scheme (see Table 5.6).

This pattern of attitudes was reinforced by the views of employees on other aspects of the schemes. Approximately two-thirds of respondents (67 per cent) indicated that their main information from schemes had come from the company's booklet and 85 per cent considered the information to be satisfactory or highly satisfactory. But of particular note was the preference for *share-based* (37 per cent) over *cash-based* (31 per cent) entitlements and the very high percentage (60 per cent) who considered that workers and managers benefited *equally* from the schemes. The latter is particularly interesting given the different benefits that managers and employees derive from schemes. (However, we have little direct evidence on employee perceptions of these diverse benefits). It is also particularly interesting that a very high percentage of respondents (58 per cent) participated in their firm's SAYE scheme. Again, as an indication of relative job security, 40 per cent considered that length of service should be the main method of calculating entitlements (though, perhaps because of the largely manual nature of the workforce, there was also a fairly high percentage (36 per cent) preferring a flat rate entitlement for employees).

Finally, there were some interesting findings in terms of respondent's attitudes towards the effects of the introduction of schemes on work patterns and on whether or not various managerial objectives had been achieved. To begin with, there was a greater spread of attitudes in both these respects than in the sample as a whole although, for the perceived effects of schemes, the 'not changed' category remained dominant. As may be seen in Table 5.7, a majority of respondents (52 per cent) identified an improvement in overall satisfaction following the introduction of schemes and a sizeable minority (34 per cent) indicated better prospects for job security. Moreover, in terms of effort put into productive work, amount of productive work done and amount of effort others put into jobs, there was a clear majority of positive over negative responses. Perhaps surprisingly, however, in terms of employee involvement and communications there were rather more negative views indicated (though this may have been because of the experience of some protracted pay negotiations prior to the interviewing period). Finally, although with respect to the success of various managerial objectives, the concentration of responses in the unsuccessful or neither successful nor unsuccessful categories was typical of the sample as a whole, it was interesting that positive

Table 5.7 A manufacturing company: employees' assessments of the effects of schemes on aspects of their work

Effects of introduction of schemes on	Decreased greatly			Not changed			Increased greatly	Other	Mean	SD
	1	2	3	4	5	6	7			
1 Overall satisfaction in working for firm	4	1	8	36	29	17	6	0	4.6	1.3
2 Feeling of job security	3	1	5	59	22	10	2	0	4.3	1.0
3 Effort put into work	1	2	6	57	18	13	4	0	4.4	1.0
4 Amount of productive work done	2	0	1	61	17	13	7	1	4.5	1.1
5 Amount of effort other people put into jobs	3	1	4	64	17	9	1	1	4.2	1.0
6 Employees' say concerning jobs	6	2	13	57	18	4	1	0	4.0	1.1
7 Employees' say in departments	4	4	10	59	16	3	1	0	3.9	1.1
8 Employees' say in overall policies of firm	6	8	9	60	15	3	1	0	3.8	1.1
9 *Your say in decisions concerning job*	8	5	4	69	12	1	1	1	3.8	1.1
10 *Your say in decisions concerning department*	7	8	3	60	14	2	1	0	3.8	1.1
11 *Your say in decisions concerning overall policies of firm*	10	2	7	75	6	4	0	1	3.6	1.1
12 Communication between management and workers	13	8	8	43	23	5	1	0	3.8	1.4

Note: Percentages, n = 104. Consistent with the questionnaire item, the scales run from negative to positive.

Table 5.8 A manufacturing company: employees' estimates of the success of schemes in terms of a number of objectives

Objectives	Very successful 1	Successful 2	Neither successful nor unsuccessful 3	Unsuccessful 4	Not at all successful 5	Don't know	No response	Mean	SD
1 To make employees more profit conscious/more interested in the company's success	1	4	35	50	9	2	0	3.7	1.0
2 To increase employees' sense of commitment to the company/make staff more liable to stay	2	3	40	46	4	5	0	3.8	1.4
3 Act as incentive to greater productivity	2	9	52	34	4	0	0	3.3	0.8
4 To make employees feel that they are part of a company – working with it, not just for it	4	8	39	44	4	1	1	3.4	1.0
5 To help to hold down wage claims	6	26	47	12	7	2	1.0	3.0	1.3
6 To provide a tax efficient means of reward									
for employees	4	12	29	39	7	6	5	3.7	1.6
for company	1	6	25	38	17	9	5	4.2	1.7
7 To ensure that employees benefit from the company's profitability	4	3	27	60	6	1	0	3.7	1.0
8 To increase employees' understanding of the financial issues that face the company	3	17	40	34	4	2	0	3.3	1.2
9 To increase the sense of cooperation between management and workforce	3	21	51	16	1	2	1	2.9	1.2

scores outweighed negative ones in the two cases of holding wage claims down and increasing the degree of cooperation between management and the workforce (see Table 5.8).

In sum, then, the manufacturing company was interested in having a coherent policy on industrial relations in which profit sharing and share ownership were an important feature. Of particular note, however, was the sustained and positive profits performance of the company which produced particularly favourable attitudes to the firm's schemes. Indeed, as we have noted, the attitudes of the predominantly manual and unionized respondents were *more* positive to profit sharing than the largely non-manual employees of the finance sector firm. They were also more prone to accept that both management and the workforce had benefited equally from the schemes and that share- rather than cash-based entitlements were an appropriate means of allocation. The importance of a firm maintaining a positive profits performance so far as employee attitudes to profit-sharing and share-ownership schemes are concerned has thus again been underlined by this particular case study.

Case 3: A retail company

The third contrasting case selected for examination is in the retail sector and is a non-union firm. Since 1980 it experienced a sharp decline in its labour force which was cut by half from over 1,300 employees in that year to only 650 employees in 1986. During the same period the original family which owned the firm lost control of the company though, as noted earlier, it still had by far the largest percentage of share capital of any group (45 per cent). Since 1980, there had also been a major reorganization of the company and repeated references were made to a change from the 'paternalistic' attitudes which prevailed prior to 1980 and the move to a more competitive market oriented approach in the recent period.

So far as profit sharing and share ownership are concerned, the APS scheme of the company is of relatively recent origin (it was introduced in December 1985), although the SAYE scheme preceded this development (being established in 1982). The company was also intending to introduce an ESO scheme. However, the relatively late development of the profit-sharing scheme may be readily understood, given the major changes in the company in the early 1980s and the financial problems it experienced in that period resulting, as has been noted, in a major cost cutting exercise and a substantial decline in the workforce.

The original managerial objectives in introducing profit-sharing and share-ownership schemes were incorporated in a booklet and these focused on the importance of giving employees 'a stake in the company' and being 'personally concerned about its profitability'. Again, however, some diverse perceptions about the objectives of profit sharing emerged from different personnel within management. The company secretary emphasized the value of schemes in terms of their encouragement of a greater consciousness of the need to make profits. The personnel manager doubted whether they would have such an effect and saw their origins and development in terms of the change in company 'culture' and the different approach to employees that this had engendered. The manager of a depot (*ie* a line manager) and also a trustee of the APS scheme saw the objectives of profit sharing in terms of an *additional* financial reward for employees and in leading to a more cost-conscious workforce concerned with reducing waste. Again, these differing perceptions should not be regarded as necessarily competing but rather as having been selected from a number of aims and focused by the particular concerns of the occupants of the varying specializations and roles within management itself.

Turning to the financial performance of the company, in Table 5.9 data are presented for the period when the firm became publicly quoted. It shows a marked improvement in profits, earnings per share, net ordinary dividends per share and turnover from the very low base of 1982. As has been mentioned, 1980–1 was a particularly traumatic period for the company, involving substantial job losses. But by 1985 and 1986 new employees were again being recruited. Against this background the late adoption of the APS scheme can be readily understood (profits needed improving before profit sharing became a meaningful exercise). Arguably, too, the earlier establishment of the SAYE scheme (involving very little cost to the company as opposed to more broadly-based profit sharing) is also interpretable in part in terms of the financial circumstances of the company in the 1980s.

Table 5.9 A retail company: profits before tax, earnings and net ordinary dividend per share, and annual turnover

Year	Profits before tax £m	Earnings per 20p share	Net ordinary dividend per 20p share	Turnover
1982	157	3.2	2.2	8,233
1983	502	11.8	3.6	11,040
1984	649	15.7	4.8	16,789
1985	1,016	20.6	5.0	18,112
1986	1,212	25.0	5.8	19,576

Turning, to the attitudes of the employees, the typical support in the sample as a whole for profit-sharing and share-ownership schemes in general was reflected in this retailing firm. Indeed, 75 per cent of respondents favoured profit sharing with cash rewards, 81 per cent supported profit sharing through shares in the company and 59 per cent endorsed Save As You Earn share-ownership schemes. Moreover, there appeared to be some satisfaction with the firm's own schemes in terms of the rewards accruing to employees: 46 per cent of respondents indicated that the APS scheme was either satisfactory or highly satisfactory and 54 per cent expressed similar views on the SAYE scheme (see Table 5.10). However, these levels of satisfaction were not as high as in the case of the brewing company and, given the different financial backgrounds of the firms, this was scarcely surprising. So far as information on schemes is concerned, 44 per cent of respondents indicated that they received this from a special memo and 35 per cent from the company booklet. Moreover, 24 per cent considered this information to be highly satisfactory, while a further 35 per cent regarded it as satisfactory (only 12 per cent viewed it as either unsatisfactory or highly unsatisfactory). Interestingly, too, 51 per cent of respondents considered that managers and workers had benefited equally from the schemes (only 22 per cent regarded managers as the main beneficiaries). Moreover, this generally favourable set of attitudes was also reinforced by the preference of employees in this firm (against the pattern in the sample as a whole) for share-based (33 per cent) over cash-based (27 per cent) schemes. And 27 per cent of respondents participated in their firm's SAYE scheme.

But were the non-unionized employees in the retail sector company distinctive in their assessment of the effects of schemes on aspects of their work and of the success of schemes in terms of achieving managerial objectives? Although our sample of employees in this firm was not large (n = 63) there did seem to be a tendency for respondents to be: (a) more positive in their estimates of the success of schemes on various aspects of their work; but (b) to be particularly sceptical about whether various managerial objectives in introducing schemes had been fulfilled.

Table 5.11 sets out the employees' perceptions of the effects of schemes on aspects of their work. Of particular note is that the majority of respondents (51 per cent) indicated improvements in overall satisfaction in working for the firm. And, although for the most part (as was the case for the sample as a whole) respondents typically indicated that there had been no change in work practices accompanying the introduction of schemes, the above average scores for improvements in job security are worth noting given the

Table 5.10 Degree of satisfaction of employees with the rewards of profit sharing and share ownership from the retail company's particular scheme

	Highly satisfactory				Highly unsatisfactory	Other/not applicable	Mean	SD
	1	2	3	4	5			
Profit sharing (APS)	5	41	29	8	0	18	2.5	0.8
Share ownership (SAYE)	11	43	19	6	0	21	2.3	0.8

Note: Percentages, n = 63.

Table 5.11 A retail company: employees' assessments of the effects of schemes on aspects of their work

Effects of introduction of schemes on	Decreased greatly			Not changed			Increased greatly	Other	Mean	SD
	1	2	3	4	5	6	7			
1 Overall satisfaction in working for firm	0	0	2	44	27	22	2	3	4.7	0.9
2 Feeling of job security	2	0	2	70	10	13	2	3	4.7	0.9
3 Effort put into work	0	0	2	68	14	10	4.5	2	4.5	0.9
4 Amount of productive work done	0	0	3	76	6	11	2	3	4.3	0.8
5 Amount of effort other people put into jobs	0	0	3	68	16	10	2	2	4.4	0.8
6 Employees' say concerning jobs	0	0	3	76	14	5	0	2	4.2	0.6
7 Employees' say in departments	0	2	0	78	14	5	0	2	4.2	0.6
8 Employees' say in overall policies of firm	0	2	0	81	11	3	2	2	4.2	0.7
9 Your say in decisions concerning job	0	0	2	83	8	5	2	2	2.0	0.6
10 Your say in decisions concerning department	0	0	3	64	14	8	0	11	4.3	0.7
11 Your say in decisions concerning overall policies of firm	0	2	3	75	6	3	0	11	4.1	0.6
12 Communication between management and workers	0	0	0	68	10	8	5	10	4.4	0.9

Note: Percentages, n = 63. Consistent with the questionnaire item, the scales run from negative to positive.

Table 5.12 A retail company: employees' estimates of the success of schemes in terms of a number of objectives

Objectives	Very successful 1	Successful 2	Neither successful nor unsuccessful 3	Unsuccessful 4	Not at all successful 5	Don't know	No response	Mean	SD
1 To make employees more profit conscious/more interested in the company's success	2	5	22	51	6	3	11	3.8	1.3
2 To increase employees' sense of commitment to the company/make staff more liable to stay	5	3	29	43	3	6	11	3.8	1.7
3 Act as incentive to greater productivity	3	5	32	40	3	5	13	3.7	1.5
4 To make employees feel that they are part of a company – working with it, not just for it	3	3	21	44	14	3	11	3.9	1.3
5 To help to hold down wage claims	5	10	57	3	2	10	14	3.5	2.1
6 To provide a tax efficient means of reward									
for employees	2	5	24	38	10	10	13	4.2	1.8
for company	2	0	22	37	13	11	16	4.5	1.9
7 To ensure that employees benefit from the company's profitability	2	3	14	51	13	6	11	4.2	1.5
8 To increase employees' understanding of the financial issues that face the company	0	8	25	38	6	10	13	4.1	1.9
9 To increase the sense of cooperation between management and workforce	3	5	44	27	5	5	11	3.6	1.5

job losses experienced by the company. Moreover, the mean scores on almost every index were slightly higher than for the sample as a whole, indicating that employees in this firm considered that schemes had been relatively effective.

The high degree of scepticism over the extent to which managerial objectives had been fulfilled by profit sharing and share ownership is of interest. The relevant information is set out in Table 5.12, where it will be noted that, with the exceptions of holding down wage claims and increasing the sense of cooperation between management and the workforce, the dominant view was that the company's schemes had been unsuccessful or not at all successful with respect to all five other issues. Moreover, relative to the sample as a whole, respondents in this particular retail firm were particularly sceptical about the effects of profit sharing on employees' loyalty to the company, productivity, making people feel they are part of a company and increasing the employees' knowledge of the financial issues that faced the company. And this may have been because of the change away from an older 'paternalistic' approach of the family-owned firm (when loyalty and commitment to the company were encouraged). Moreover, the financial problems of the firm in the early 1980s had in any event occasioned considerable concern over productivity and, in such a milieu, employees were fully aware of the consequential nature of financial issues for the wellbeing of the firm, regardless of whether or not profit-sharing schemes had been introduced. In both respects, therefore, profit sharing and share ownership were unlikely to be seen as being *by themselves* of consequence in furthering managerial objectives.

The retail company examined in the third case was thus of interest in consequence of being in a different sector, having a non-unionized workforce and having experienced considerable financial problems and job losses in the early 1980s. Moreover, the firm had experienced a substantial organizational change reflected in a movement away from the early family-owned 'paternalistic' approach and the growth of a more competitive, financially-aware enterprise with a rather different company 'culture'. These circumstances affected the experience of profit sharing by occasioning, above all, a delay in the introduction of the APS scheme. Moreover, so far as employee attitudes were concerned, although the firm's schemes were less favourably viewed than in the manufacturing concern, the good profits of the two past years or so may have led to a recognition that managers and workers had benefited equally from schemes and to a preference for the financially rewarding share-based schemes. Nevertheless, the dramatic situation of the early 1980s (which was manifested above all in a halving of the workforce) would appear to have led to a considerable measure of doubt about the effectiveness of schemes in terms of inculcating employee loyalty to the organization, not least when such characteristics in a workforce were no longer particularly valued by the management itself.

Conclusions

The data presented in this chapter thus help to reveal the complex interrelationships between the financial and economic performance of companies, the introduction of schemes and attitudes to particular types of arrangement. There is clearly an intricate and interlinked set of conditions within companies which impact upon actual practices. Detailed case study analysis has clearly helped to reveal these distinctive patterns and to amplify broader findings of a representative national survey. It is now appropriate to move on to a more detail review of the principal findings of this research project and to highlight general conclusions on the operation of profit-sharing and employee-shareholding schemes as a whole.

Chapter six

Conclusions and prospects

For upwards of a century, in countries with diverse cultures and political economies, the notion of economic democracy has been widely advocated and a variety of practices encompassed by this concept have been established. In two interrelated volumes, we have been able to focus on one of its principal manifestations: the rise of profit-sharing and employee-shareholding schemes. We have seen that interest in employee financial participation overall has become increasingly worldwide, with the acceleration of interest being particularly pronounced in the United States and the United Kingdom. By marshalling a rich range of data stemming from a research project conducted under the auspices of the British Department of Employment, it has proved to be possible to uncover the main forces promoting this development and to examine, in depth and detail, the actual impact of schemes within the company.

It is now appropriate to re-evaluate the principal findings of our enquiry and to examine the prospects for the advance of economic democracy in the years ahead. To accomplish these objectives, our conclusions embrace four main themes: (1) the theoretical analysis of economic democracy and a re-emphasis of the interrelated nature of the factors isolated in the main explanatory model of profit-sharing and share-ownership schemes; (2) an outline of key findings focusing particularly on the impact of schemes; (3) a discussion of some general implications, arguments and propositions; and (4) a brief analysis of the prospects for the future.

Theories and models

In the first volume of this enquiry, it was argued that the development of employee financial participation is best understood in terms of the notion of favourable conjunctures. That is to say, rather than a straightforward evolutionary or cyclical pattern being in evidence, the historical record is suggestive of a discontinuous but broadly advancing movement. Moreover, as we observed in Volume 1, the consolidated gains of the 1980s are, in our view, best understood against a background of facilitative legislation. Nevertheless, the *varied* pattern of adoption of schemes in companies requires a rather different explanation, with the most important factors being aspects of the economic infrastructure (the varied rates of development of different industrial sectors being relevant here), the choices of key managers reflecting distinctive styles of industrial relations, the industrial relations climate in the firm itself, and the support or otherwise of employee collectives (trade unions and staff associations).

In Volume 2, we have focused primarily upon the impact of schemes and have suggested an approach which views the adoption of profit sharing and share ownership in terms of the organizational identification of employees. This can comprise either intrinsic commitment stemming from improvements in participation, security and job satisfaction; or, alternatively, extrinsic commitment (notably improvements in instrumental rewards from work). But so far as outcomes are concerned, the impact of schemes can be assessed by reference to the financial performance of companies (profitability, productivity), industrial relations performance (reduced conflict, labour turnover and absenteeism and improved management–employee relations), and organizational performance (improved employee involvement, satisfaction with the company, and adaptability and flexibility).

From a theoretical standpoint, then, we have been able to isolate the main issues associated with the impact of schemes. However, so far as broader economic consequences of profit sharing for inflation and unemployment are concerned, we cannot add significantly to the arguments set out in the introduction. But in terms of model building, we have been able to highlight some interesting conclusions. Above all, it is clear that the impact of schemes is seldom direct and that complex interactive and multivariate interpretations of profit sharing and share ownership are essential. The consequences of schemes for financial, industrial relations and organizational performance are affected by environmental influences. And although it is possible to establish links between the adoption of schemes and favourable attitudes to the organization, again a highly interactive pattern of relationships is observable.

In theoretical terms, it is clear that simplistic cause and effect models do not in any way represent actual patterns of conduct in organizations and that complex theories of the impact of employee financial participation are required. Moreover, as we have seen, a favourable outcome so far as the impact of schemes are concerned is likely to encourage further developments in employee financial participation itself.

The impact of schemes

Turning, more specifically, at this point to assess the impact of schemes, we are able to offer some insightful conclusions on the links between the adoption of profit sharing and share ownership and the financial, industrial relations and organizational performance of companies. To begin with, there is almost certainly a positive relationship between company profitability and whether or not a firm has adopted profit-sharing schemes. However, there remains considerable doubt about the direction of this relationship. In particular, our data suggest that an improved profits performance is frequently the trigger mechanism for the adoption of schemes. This, in turn, enables a company to continue an onward advance in terms of profitability (not least because there are no negative effects of making substantial profits and not sharing these adequately with the workforce). But the time series data available to us showed that there was no direct necessary linkage between the adoption of schemes and an accelerated profits performance. And any effects here may be counterbalanced by environmental conditions (such as exchange rate movements, oil price fluctuations, interest rates and so on). In short, our evidence suggests a highly complex and intertwined relationship between profit sharing and profitability. *Ceteris paribus*, firms introducing schemes can expect positive financial consequences, though these may well be indirect and mediated through organizational identification and commitment. But there is not a direct linear relationship here or any certainty that firms introducing schemes will inevitably reap substantial financial benefits.

The same general conclusions apply to industrial relations performance. Firms frequently introduce schemes as part of an attempt to improve their industrial relations climate, but our evidence suggests a complex pattern of relationships. Indeed, well-managed companies, with consultative-type employee relations policies, are in any case likely to experience lower levels of strikes and absenteeism and to have profit-sharing-type schemes. Indeed, it is clear from our interviews with key respondents and from data on strikes and absenteeism that the nature of a given industry could be particularly important in affecting outcomes. There were also some indications (though much of these were impressionistic) that labour turnover is reduced by the introduction of schemes. And certainly one of the managerial objectives for adopting both APS and ESO schemes is to reduce labour turnover. But some types of industry (*eg* clothing, retailing) have high rates of labour turnover in any case and these are unlikely to be dramatically reduced by profit-sharing and employee-shareholding schemes. Indeed, the most important impact of profit sharing is almost certainly to improve organizational identification and commitment and hence, indirectly, to enhance industrial relations performance. But to expect a direct causal relationship between these variables is in our view unrealistic, and it is in any event not one which is by and large anticipated by the initiators of the schemes themselves.

The link between profit sharing, and employee shareholding and attitudes, rather than behaviour, was reinforced by an analysis of the impact of schemes on organizational performance. In our survey of the views of employees, we discovered that, while comparatively few respondents indicated that their productive work had noticeably increased following the introduction of schemes, both communications and satisfaction in working for the company had shown a far more marked improvement. Moreover, attitudes to schemes for profit sharing and share ownership were found to be interlinked with positive views on the firm itself. In short, the strategy of improving the climate of management–employee relations by means of economic democracy would appear to be very soundly based and it is an important conclusion of our study as a whole.

General implications

The theoretical approach adopted in this enquiry and the data presented on the origins and impact of schemes for profit sharing and employee share ownership should, it is hoped, have shed light on an issue of current moment in political and economic debate. But, at this concluding juncture in our two volume study, there are a number of more general arguments and propositions which merit more detailed appraisal. These are: (1) the notion of a transformation of capitalist economies to property owning democracies; (2) the analytical significance and potency in economic development of the firm rather than the state or the market; (3) the salience of managerial style in the genesis and operation of schemes; (4) the complexities of practice and the importance of differentiating between the main forms of employee financial participation; (5) the international character of the movement towards economic democracy; and (6) the interlinked nature of the forms of organizational democracy itself.

The first general argument to be addressed is to what extent does employee financial participation contribute to the establishment of a so called property owning democracy? The case here has been cogently articulated by Copeman, Moore and Arrowsmith (1984), who have noted the productive power of the capitalist system and its ability to generate a high level of income for its participants. But, in their view, capital concentration has remained so high that it has proved to be 'the Achilles heel of the free enterprise system – the shutting out of employees from participation in the businesses' where they work (Copeman, Moore and Arrowsmith, 1984: 15). And this in turn may well have contributed to the growth of political philosophies aimed at destroying the free enterprise system.

For our part, although we have no direct evidence on the relationship (if one is present at all) between employee shareholding and the adoption of particular political philosophies, we are reasonably certain that the *current* extent and depth of employee financial participation is not sufficient to have such transformative qualities. More specifically, we have found that share ownership does not appear to have breached a predominant 'employee consciousness'. None the less, employees undoubtedly welcome share ownership and their chances of purchasing shares in companies other than those in which they are employed has improved substantially in recent years. Moreover, ownership of shares *is* linked with other sets of attitudes and hence, leaving to one side the problems over the direction of this relationship, there may be a slow evolutionary change along the lines predicted by Copeman, Moore and Arrowsmith (1984). But a fundamental shift in employee attitudes to work, employment and society would require a far more extensive movement involving substantially greater shareholdings by employees than is currently the case.

Another intriguing argument which has developed around the notion of profit sharing has been the recognition of the firm as a key force in economic development. This in turn, implies a greater analytical significance for the enterprise rather than for the state or the market in explaining different patterns of advance in modern industrial societies. As Rosen, Klein and Young (1986) have observed:

After all these years of worshipping at the altar of Smith, Marx or Keynes, here is a whole new paradigm. Neither the market nor the state, nor even some combination, must assume the mythic dimensions and capabilities they often do in conventional theories. Instead, the firm becomes the vehicle for both economic growth and social justice.

This is a proposition to which organizational behaviour and industrial relations scholars have been committed for a substantial period; but the focus on the 'shared economy' has reinvigorated a longstanding debate. Certainly our view is that an analysis at the level of the firm is essential for understanding the diverse patterns of development of profit sharing and share ownership. It is at the level of the enterprise that the key decisions to embark upon profit sharing and share ownership are formulated in the first place. And although these decisions are influenced by wider environmental exigencies, there is considerable choice, not only in the decision on whether or not to adopt a scheme, but also the specific arrangements which are selected. Moreover, the impact of different schemes is also affected by a wide range of intra-organizational variables.

These broader arguments on the importance of the firm are linked with the recognition of the impact of managerial strategy and style in the adoption and operation of schemes for employee financial participation and for economic development more generally. Indeed, increasingly it has been understood that effective management at the level of the firm is basic to actual outcomes in a range of economic, social and industrial relations issues. For our part, the evidence presented in two volumes undoubtedly reinforces such a viewpoint. The managements of particular companies largely decide on whether or not to introduce schemes and on the details of the schemes adopted. The communications systems in companies which convey information are ultimately structured by the managements in particular firms. And the preferred style of management (and above all the support for consultative and employee involvement practices generally) is basic to understanding the genesis and operation of several forms of employee financial participation.

None the less, it is important to note that employee financial participation is a highly complex phenomenon. Broadly speaking, it is possible to identify a number of levels of economic democracy ranging from managerial equity and executive profit sharing, to employee equity and all-employee schemes for profit sharing, to capital sharing and finally to pure economic democracy itself in which there is ownership of the enterprise by all the members of the firm (see Volume 1). But in every one of these general types, there are substantial variations and a number of different approaches. Some of the complications, such as with ESOPs, have arisen from the requirement to balance public, employee and employer interests. Others have developed from diverse managerial, employee or trade union strategies at the level of the firm. In the case of profit-sharing and employee-ownership schemes there is a choice over whether to adopt cash- or share-based schemes (or a combination of both). Decisions have then to be taken over whether or not to develop Inland Revenue approved schemes and to trade off financial benefits against various restrictions such as those imposed by Investment Protection Committees. Further choices over APS or SAYE schemes have also to be made in UK companies. And international variations in practice make the patterns of development more complex.

An important general conclusion of our study is thus that profit-sharing and employee-shareholding schemes have highly diverse origins and modes of operation. Moreover, this is undoubtedly a consequential issue because it implies that there are not only different forces which underlie the growth of particular schemes (*eg* the APS or SAYE types of arrangement) but also diverse effects in terms of employee commitment, improved financial or industrial relations performance and so on which are implicit in the various approaches.

A further issue to be addressed is to what extent the development of profit sharing and employee shareholding is confined to countries such as the USA and UK and to what extent it is a genuinely international movement. There is no doubt that interest in this phenomenon has become widespread and that developments have been rapid in North America and Europe in the 1980s. Moreover, particular types (such as the ESOPs) have become especially important as focal models for advances which have taken place outside their countries of origin. The Swedish commitment to capital sharing via Meidner plans has also been an influential approach. Nevertheless, there remains considerable diversity in international practice both in terms of the extent of development of profit sharing and employee shareholding and in the actual types of practice adopted (the low levels of interest in West Germany until recently being particularly noteworthy in this respect). However, it is our considered view that developments in profit sharing and share ownership on a worldwide scale are likely to become increasingly marked in the years ahead. This is partly because of the improved competitiveness of companies which introduce schemes, but also because of current transformations in organization and technology. After all, these are impelling firms to promote a variety of programmes in human resource management in order to attract and retain an adaptable core workforce to meet the requirements of emergent markets and their continuous and rapid change. Hence, while diversity in actual practice is likely to remain characteristic, there is every reason to suppose that profit sharing and employee share ownership will become increasingly global in compass.

But how far, it may be reasonably asked, is economic democracy linked with industrial democracy and with the more general advance of organizational democracy itself?

The ideal of working men and women participating in and having a financial stake in the companies in which they are employed has of course captured the intellectual imagination for upwards of a century and has been particularly pronounced in the post-war period. In Volume 1, we were able to demonstrate that firms which introduce a variety of types of financial participation also tend to be those with relatively advanced practices for involving employees in other aspects of the company's affairs. They are also likely to reach decisions on industrial relations issues after consultation or negotiation with the workforce. Further links have been demonstrated in this volume and, above all, we have found that employee shareholders typically have a greater say in how their jobs are done and that share ownership is strongly linked with a *desire* for greater influence over decision-making. This was found to apply to the overall policies of the firm, as well as to matters affecting an individual's department and how the job itself is actually done. So long as the modes of employee involvement are cognate, therefore, there are strong grounds for concluding that the various types of organizational democracy advance in parallel.

The future

Does this suggest that further substantial movements towards greater employee financial and decision-making involvement are likely to develop in the years ahead? Our conclusions in this respect must be cautiously optimistic. There is no inexorable evolutionary trend towards organizational democracy but the 'favourable conjunctures' of circumstance which have fuelled the growth of employee financial participation in the 1980s will almost certainly be augmented. Accompanying demographic changes, acute shortages of labour may well be evident in the advancing sectors of the economy and this will impel managements to formulate a variety of human resource strategies (including the introduction of share-based schemes) in order to ensure the maintenance of an adaptable, flexible and committed workforce. So far as competitiveness is concerned, it is seldom fully appreciated that comparatively small advantages in terms of improvements in employee attitudes and behaviour can have highly significant long-term consequences in the international marketplace. And, in this respect, the positive consequences of the introduction of profit-sharing and share-ownership schemes for employee attitudes and behaviour may not only be more substantial than is commonly supposed but may also be sufficient to ensure an insistent and continuous pressure for further advances in the future.

None the less, progress is likely to remain uneven in different countries and across the various employment sectors. Unless there is mandatory legislation, employee financial and decision-making involvement will not be universal features of the modern industrial and post-industrial societies. While they may not be a panacea for all economic, industrial relations and organizational problems, the prospects for a growth in economic or industrial democracy in the years ahead are undoubtedly favourable. Hence our conclusion must be that, notwithstanding the diverse rationales for the advance, a variety of types of organizational democracy is likely to become increasingly widespread, not only in the 1990s, but above all in the twenty-first century when the various and diverse supportive conditions have come to their full fruition.

Case studies

The main aim of this volume has been to outline the principal findings of the case study phase of the Department of Employment sponsored project on profit sharing and share ownership and to assess the theoretical and empirical evidence on the potential impact of profit-sharing and share-ownership schemes in the UK.

The objectives of the case studies were:

(1) to obtain detailed and accurate information on the processes involved in setting up schemes and the managerial objectives in introducing them;

(2) to examine the relationship of schemes with the financial and industrial relations performance of companies, their degree of success (and the factors associated with this);

(3) to assess the role schemes play in relation to other employee involvement practices; and

(4) to identify and explore any obstacles to the development of profit sharing and share ownership.

In the design of the research, it was considered especially important to obtain information on employee views and on company performance as well as extending interviews with key respondents to include personnel in a number of managerial functions and in trade unions. In particular, the following research design was proposed:

(1) To select about 20 case studies, covering a variety of companies, drawn from the Stage 1 sample in consultation with IFF Research Limited (the survey contractor).

(2) At least 14 of the case study companies would be operating all-employee Inland Revenue Approved schemes. The other cases would include companies with other types of profit sharing, or with schemes for specific groups of employees (including Executive Share Option (ESO) schemes), or with no schemes at all.

(3) At least six of the case study companies would have recent schemes (*ie* ones introduced prior to spring 1986); the others would include companies with schemes in existence for more than three years.
(4) Detailed interviews would take place with key management respondents (*eg* financial managers, personnel/industrial relations managers and line managers) and with trade union representatives.
(5) Information on company performance (including economic and industrial relations indicators) would be obtained, preferably over a ten year period.
(6) In general, the case studies were not meant to provide quantitative data since these had been provided by the overall survey in Stage 1. However, it was considered important to gauge employee opinion by means of a self-completed questionnaire. This included personnel at all levels in the organization. This part of the research was conducted at establishment level (by contrast with interviews with key managerial respondents, which were more typically at company headquarters). It was thus decided to carry out case study work both at company headquarter and at establishment levels.

In order to accomplish these objectives, there were thus three main parts to the case study phase: (1) interviews with key personnel; (2) the gathering of data on company performance; and (3) an employee attitude survey. Some of the important issues covered in each section are highlighted below.

(1) Interviews with key personnel

These were based on a semi-structured interview schedule and involved obtaining information from managers directly involved in the establishment and/or administration of profit-sharing/share-ownership schemes. Full details of the schedule are included in Appendix 2.
The data gathered from the management schedule included:

Detailed information on types of scheme adopted.
Views on legislation and possible changes.
A detailed exploration of the objectives of schemes.
A detailed assessment by respondents of problems encountered in the operation of schemes.
Information on how employees leave schemes, taxation, the

nature of employee shareholdings and the role of the
Investment Protection Committees.
A detailed analysis of links with other forms of employee
involvement.
An assessment of the effects of schemes on profitability,
employee adaptability, industrial relations practices and
workforce attitudes.

The views of trade union representatives were also examined.
Indeed, a specific schedule was designed for this purpose and
included questions on the assessment of the various types of Inland
Revenue Approved schemes: profit-sharing schemes (APS), Save
As You Earn share-ownership schemes (SAYE), and Executive
Share Option schemes (ESO), and their effects (see Appendix 3).
We also sought to establish whether trade unions had formulated
any general policies on profit sharing and share ownership.

(2) Data on company performance ('behavioural data')

In order to make some further assessment of the relationship of
schemes with the financial and industrial relations performance of
companies, data were also gathered on a number of relevant issues.
These are referred to as 'behavioural data' to distinguish them
from material based on the *viewpoints* of management and
employees. The data here include annual absenteeism rates, annual
labour turnover, annual company turnover/sales, annual profits,
industrial disputes, annual net dividend per share and annual
capital–labour ratio. So far as possible data were gathered over the
last ten years.

(3) Employee attitudes

A key part of this phase of the research was of course to obtain
information on employee attitudes (see questionnaire – Appendix
4). The questions were designed to elicit employee views on profit-
sharing and share-ownership schemes generally, experience within
employing companies, the success or otherwise of schemes,
information on schemes and how satisfactory this has been, and
preferences for particular type of scheme and modes of distribution
of profits. More specifically, too, we sought detailed information
to assess the link identified in the survey phase of the research
between these schemes and employee involvement more generally.

The case study companies

In order to carry out the research it was necessary to select approximately 20 case study companies for detailed exploration. These were drawn from the 303 'main stage' firms of Phase 1 of the project and were included to reflect variations in types of schemes, the periods when particular schemes were introduced, the size of enterprise, industrial sector and degree of unionization. In March 1986, over 40 cases were selected from the data at IFF Research Limited. IFF Research Limited then sent a standard letter to the companies involved to seek cooperation for the case study phase. If this was forthcoming, details of the company and a key respondent were passed on to the UWCC research team which then arranged initial headquarters visits. Ultimately, it proved to be feasible to obtain information from 22 cases in this way, divided roughly equally between London/South East of England and South Wales/ the South West of England and providing a good coverage of the varying characteristics of companies with respect to size, sector, unionization and so on. It was considered important to examine the experiences of firms in London/South East of England because Stage 1 suggested that companies in this region were particularly likely to have schemes; South Wales provided a valuable contrast since this region has had traditional heavy industries with a substantial degree of public sector employment. And, although this situation has been rapidly changing in recent years, with the establishment of new types of industry (particularly in electronics) and a variety of financial and service sector activities, there are still likely to be differences in the types of workplace in the two regions, which may have relevance to attitudes to profit sharing and share ownership.

Full details of the case study companies in these respects are set out in Table A1. For each of the firms, information is presented on type of scheme, date of introduction of scheme, the existence or otherwise of other related incentive schemes, industrial sector, size of organization (measured by number of employees) and extent of unionization.

So far as type of scheme is concerned, it will be noted that 17 firms have APS schemes, 14 firms approved SAYE schemes and 16 firms approved ESO schemes. In addition, two firms had no approved schemes at all, and one firm had no APS scheme but, at the time of the interviews, was in the process of applying for Inland Revenue approval for its SAYE and ESO schemes. However, there is no neat division between firms with approved and non-approved schemes, which typically run in parallel with the approved schemes.

Table A1 The case study companies

| Company | Approved | | | | | | Not approved | Other incentive schemes | Industrial sector | Number of employees | Unionization percentage | | |
	APS (S53) FA 1978 (trust)	Date introduced	SAYE (S47) FA 1980 (saving)	Date introduced	ESO (S36) FA 1984 (selected)	Date introduced					Blue	White	Total
A*	Yes	1983	Yes	1982	Yes	1984			Manufacturing	580	55	90	72
B	Yes	1983	Yes	1986	No	1986			Distribution	6,872	100	99	95
C*	No		No		No		ESO 1982		Services	260	No unions		
D	Yes	May 1984	Yes	Oct 1984	Yes	Oct 1984	ESO 1972	Cash bonus scheme 1980–5	Manufacturing	11,622	90	80	85
E*	Yes	Nov 1979	No		Yes	1984	Profit-sharing scheme 1970s		Finance	470	No unions		
F*	Yes	1984	Yes	1984	Yes	1986	SAYE and ESO 1975		Manufacturing	3,700	No unions		
G	Yes	1985	Yes	1981	No				Retail	5,616	49	92	71
H*	No		Applying		Applying		SAYE and ESO 1982		Finance	7,000	—	—	65
I	Yes	1979	Applying		Yes	1984	PS 1976–9 ESO 1976–84		Retail	10,959	No unions		
J	No		Yes	1985	No		ESO 1979		Finance	3,000 (UK)	No unions		
K*	Yes	1980	Yes	1984	Yes	1984	PS 1954 SAYE 1979		Manufacturing	57,200	100	40	70

Firm							Scheme		Sector	Employees	Unions	
L*	Yes	1979	Yes	1983	Yes	1984	ESO 1971 1978–84		Service	6,000	No unions —	50
M	Yes	1982	Yes	1981	Yes	1985	SAYE 1974 and 1983 ESO 1974 PS 1978		Finance	5,909	— —	
N*	Yes	1980	Yes	1982	Yes	Dec 1984	ESO 1980		Other	122	No unions —	
O*	Yes	1979	Yes	1981	Yes	1985	SAYE 1979 ESO 1979		Finance	50,000	— —	50
P	Yes	1980	No	1980	Yes	1984			Finance	580	No unions	
Q*	Yes	Dec 1985	Yes	1982	Yes	1985		Sales staff bonus scheme	Retail	650	No unions	
R	Yes	1980	No	1980	Yes	1984			Services	421	10 —	4
S	No		Yes	1986	Yes	1986			Services	1,278	No unions	
T	No	1980	No		No	1985			Other	115	— —	50
U*	Yes	1980	No	1980	Yes	1985	ESO 1971 and 1981 SAYE 1975		Manufacturing	42,750	— —	55
V	Yes	1985	Yes	1980	Yes	1984	SAYE 1976–80 ESO 1976–84		Finance	2,800	No unions	

Note: * Firms which participated in the employee questionnaire part of the research. NB A further company in the service sector was added which was in the Stage I sample but did not feature in terms of interviews with key respondents and the gathering of behavioural data.

There is also a good representation of early and recent schemes amongst the case study companies: 13 of the approved APS or SAYE schemes had been introduced in 1981 or earlier and 11 had been adopted in 1984 or later (6 in 1985 or 1986). The distribution of firms by sector is as follows: finance (7), manufacturing (5), services (4), retail/distribution (4), other (2).

Companies of varied size and patterns of unionization are also included amongst the case studies. Thus, while 8 companies have fewer than 1,000 employees, 5 have more than 10,000 employees, with the balance of companies between these two figures. Eleven companies have no trade unions at all. Amongst those with unions, the levels of union density range between 4 per cent and 95 per cent (see again Table A1).

Interviews with key personnel

Following the selection of firms, interviews with key respondents were arranged at headquarters level. In all the case study companies, a full schedule was completed with at least one manager at this level. Typically, however, we sought a spread of headquarters managers (covering the company secretary/director of finance and group personnel manager) and establishment-level managers. There were considerable variations amongst the cases depending on management structure. After all, in the smallest firms, there was only a relatively limited degree of specialization of management functions and there was typically only one establishment. However, in the largest companies, roles were well defined and it was necessary to visit a number of establishments: (a) to carry out more detailed interviews with line managers/site personnel officers; (b) to contact union representatives in the unionized companies; and, (c) most important of all, to arrange for the distribution of employee questionnaires. So far as the main schedule is concerned (see Appendix 2), this was administered to a minimum of one and a maximum of 14 key respondents in the various case study firms.

Following the interviews with headquarters key respondents, we then entered into consultations on appropriate sites for distributing questionnaires and carrying out further interviews (including, where relevant, with union representatives). At this point, we did meet with some resistance from managements unwilling to allow us to survey employee attitudes but we were able to undertake this exercise in twelve companies. So far as trade union representatives are concerned, approximately 25 representatives were interviewed in the following unions: AEU, ASTMS, BIFU, CPSA, IPCS, NUTGW and TGWU. Moreover, seven full-time officers outside the firms were interviewed (notably in ASTMS, BIFU, GMBATU and TGWU).

Company performance indicators

Key respondents at headquarters level were also asked to provide details on company performance covering both financial and industrial relations issues. However, whilst it proved possible to obtain a full set of information on annual profits after tax, annual turnover/sales, annual capital−labour ratio and annual earnings per share, the data on industrial relations performance were not so complete. For the number of stoppages per company this was scarcely surprising (after all, in any given year, the majority of British companies do not have strikes). But for annual absenteeism rates and annual labour turnover, although it was possible to make a number of inter-firm comparisons, the data supplied were far from comprehensive: (a) because some companies did not gather statistics of this type; (b) because in others the information applied variously to company *or* establishment level but not both; and (c) because some firms were prepared to provide these data for only a single year.

Employee questionnaires

The aim of the questionnaires was to elicit employee views at all levels in the organization and the distribution was based on one or more establishments in a given company. The number of question-naires distributed varied according to the size of company and was designed to produce roughly 2,000 completed schedules overall. It was necessary to vary the contents of questionnaires slightly (particularly with respect to the section on trade unions) but, apart from this set of questions, relatively few modifications were suggested by management or union at establishment/headquarters levels.

The final total of employee questionnaires (1,931) is based on distributions in twelve companies with the establishments carefully selected to provide a roughly equal number of respondents in the London/South East of England and the South Wales/South West of England regions. Apart from establishments in London, in the first mentioned region, sites in Luton, Ipswich, Maidstone and Brighton were all included. Moreover, in South Wales/South West of England, establishments covered not only those based in Cardiff and Bristol, but also Pontypool, Weston-super-Mare, Gloucester, Swansea, Magor, Newport and Merthyr Tydfil.

Table A2 Distribution of respondents by sector, region and firm size

Sector	Manufacturing	Services	Finance	Retail/distribution	Other
Number of respondents	487	377	976	63	28
Number of firms	4	2	3	1	2

Region	South Wales/South West	London/South East
Number of respondents	985	946

Firm size	2,500 employees or under	Over 2,500 employees
Number of respondents	437	1,494

In Table A2, the distribution of respondents by sector, region and firm size is set out. It will be seen that the largest single group of respondents (976) is in the finance sector, followed by manufacturing (487), services (377), retail/distribution (63) and other (28). This is a reasonable reflection of the experience in Britain as a whole since, proportionately, the highest penetration of schemes is in the finance sector. Indeed, on the basis of Stage 1 findings, 50 per cent of companies in the finance sector had all employee schemes, followed by services (30 per cent), manufacturing (21 per cent), retail/distribution (13 per cent) and other (12 per cent). It will also be noted in Table A2 that the regional distribution of respondents is 985 (South Wales/South West) and 946 (London/South East). About one quarter of respondents are employed in firms with 2,500 employees or fewer and three quarters in larger concerns. Again, this is not an unreasonable balance since the larger publicly-quoted companies are particularly likely to have schemes.

Check list
Interviews with key respondents

Check list

In each case study data is sought under the following three headings:

1 Interviews with key personnel

Interviews will be conducted with key personnel in the company, *ie* senior management closely involved with share schemes, the personnel manager(s) and a senior employee representative(s). The numbers of key personnel interviews will be determined by the size of the workforce. Interviews will be conducted with the help of a semi-structured interview schedule to ensure comparability of data between companies. In addition, supporting documentation in the form of annual reports, brochures, policy documents, minutes etc, will be obtained where permissible.

2 Behavioural data

Behavioural data will be acquired from each case study to identify changes in company over the last ten years. This will include the following:

a) Present number of full-time and part-time employees broken down by sex, age, length of service, status and income.
b) Annual absenteeism rate.
c) Annual labour turnover.
d) Annual turnover/sales.
e) Annual profits.
f) Number of disputes/stoppages per annum, numbers involved and duration.
g) Annual net dividend per share.
h) Annual capital−labour ratio.

3 *Employee attitudes*

An employee questionnaire will be distributed to at least 10 per cent of employees in each case study to obtain broad views on profit-sharing and share-ownership schemes.

Key personnel semi-structured interview schedule

1 *Type of schemes*

a) Which scheme do you operate?
  i) ADST (Approved Deferred Share Trust)
  ii) SAYE (Save As You Earn)
  iii) Cash based
  iv) Share based
  v) Mixed
  vi) Executive Share Option Scheme
b) Where and how did you hear about these schemes?
c) When were these schemes introduced? Who were the key people setting them up?
d) Have there been any recent changes in the schemes, *eg* Budget 1986?
e) Are you in the process of introducing a scheme?
f) Were there any administrative problems in setting up these schemes?

2 *Legislation*

a) Is the present legislation easy to understand – by company/ employees?
b) Should the legislation be simplified?
c) What (other) changes to the legislation would you make (if any)?
d) Have there been any problems regarding approval by:
  i) The Inland Revenue?
  ii) The Investment Protection Committees?
e) Were there any problems regarding the time taken to get approval?

3 *Objectives*

a) What were your objectives in introducing these schemes?
b) Were there any other objectives you considered? What were they?

Interviewer only – Probe

   i) As an alternative Industrial Relations strategy? ADST
SAYE ESO
   ii) As a tax efficient means of rewarding employees?
   iii) To make employees more cost, and profit conscious?
   iv) To compete with other firms?
   v) As part of general Employee Involvement policy?
   vi) To keep down/substitute for wage increases?
   vii) To deter official/unofficial industrial action?
   viii) To increase loyalty/sense of commitment to the firm?

c) Have your objectives been met? If so, can you give an
example?
d) Since introducing the scheme have you modified your
objectives?
e) What are the advantages of the schemes to the company/
employee?
f) Are there any disadvantages you would like to mention?

4 Share Option Schemes (SAYE)

a) What is the minimum period shares must be left in scheme –
5 or 7 years?
b) Who is eligible for the scheme? How did you decide on these
criteria? Do they relate back to the objectives? Should they be
changed, *eg* do you think they should be all embracing? Do
they include part-timers?
c) How many employees have joined the scheme? Percentage of
those eligible? Average saved? Length of option? Bonus other
than tax concessions?
d) How is the individual share calculated? What is the average
individual share?
e) Are there any limits on an individual share/savings? What are
the maximum share earnings? What is the maximum saving?
f) What is the option price of the share? How many options?
Percentage discount?
g) How much has been paid out to date?
h) What are the advantages of your scheme to company/
employees?
i) Are there any disadvantages?
j) What changes, if any, would you make?

5 Executive Share Option Scheme

a) What sort of scheme is on offer?
b) Who is eligible? Why did you decide on this criteria?
c) How many participated? Percentage of those eligible?
d) Is there any relationship between this and any other scheme?
e) Are the objectives for this scheme considerably different from the other schemes, or is it just an extension of the same principle?
f) Are there any limits on the individual share? What are they?
g) What changes, if any, would you make?
h) What is the option price of the shares? How many options? Percentage discounts?
i) Are there any disadvantages?

6 Profit Sharing Schemes (ADST)

a) Who are the trustees in the scheme?
b) Is one of the trustees a senior union/staff association representative?
c) How is the profit distributed under this scheme?
d) Is the distribution in the form of cash, shares or both?
e) Is this arrangement satisfactory?
f) Who is eligible for the scheme? How did you decide on these criteria? Do they relate back to the objectives? Should they be changed? *Eg* do you think they should be all embracing? Do they include part-timers?
g) How many employees have joined the scheme? Percentage of those eligible?
h) What is the minimum period shares must be left in trust?
i) Are there any limits on the individual share? What are they?
j) How many shares have been allotted? Total value of shares in trust? Percentage of total share value?
k) What are the advantages of your scheme to company/ employees?
l) Are there any disadvantages?
m) What changes, if any, would you make?

7 Leaving the scheme

a) What arrangements are there for those who leave the scheme?
b) Are those arrangements satisfactory from the company/ employee point of view?

8 Taxation

a) What are the tax advantages/disadvantages for your employee/company?
b) What improvements would you like to see regarding tax concessions for employees/company?

9 Shares

a) Should employee shares be differentiated from ordinary shares?
b) Have there been any problems regarding the market value of shares?
c) Should there be a link between employee and executive shares?

10 Investment Protection Committees

a) Were the IPC restrictions an important consideration in setting up schemes?
b) Are these restrictions satisfactory?
c) What changes, if any, would you like to see?

11 Employee involvement

a) Do you have an overall industrial relations policy in the company? What contribution does profit sharing/share ownership make to this policy?
b) Are there any unions/staff associations which are recognized by your company? Which?
c) Percentage of employees those unions/staff associations represent? Which employees?
d) What collective bargaining and consultative arrangements do you have with these unions/staff associations? How do these impact upon profit sharing?
e) Are any of the schemes negotiable? Is this compatible with overall industrial relations policy?
f) Were the trade unions/staff associations consulted before the introduction of the schemes?
g) How did you inform your employees of the schemes – directly, through union/staff association channels? What mode did this take? Did employees find this satisfactory?
h) Were there any difficulties in understanding the schemes?
i) Have you continued to inform employees/advise them on the schemes subsequent to setting them up?

j) Should employee shareholders have the same voting rights as ordinary shareholders? What voting rights do they have at the moment?

k) Was there any discernible opposition to the schemes from:
    i) Trade union/staff association?
    ii) Employees generally?
    iii) Shareholders?
    iv) Others?

l) Have you had any other feedback on the schemes from any of these?

m) Has financial participation by employees:
    i) increased profitability through improved efficiency?
    ii) made organizational changes more acceptable by employees?
    iii) reduced levels of absenteeism, labour turnover?
    iv) improved employee attitudes at work?

n) What other forms of employee involvement are there in the company? To what extent do these link with profit sharing/share ownership?

o) Has the introduction of the scheme(s) affected/changed company employee involvement policy?

Trade union representatives
Semi-structured interview schedule

1 Schemes – union policy

a) Does your union have a policy on profit-sharing/share-ownership schemes? National policy? District or Branch policy?
   If no, do you think there is a need for such a policy?
   If yes, have there been any recent changes in that policy?
b) Has the introduction of the schemes in this company caused any problems for you or your members?
c) What are the major advantages/disadvantages of the scheme for your members?

2 Legislation

a) Are you aware of the recent legislation on profit-sharing and share-ownership schemes (*ie* Finance Acts 1978, 1980 and 1984)?
   If yes, do you think this legislation is easy to understand?
b) What changes would you like to see in the legislation?

3 Objectives of management

a) What were the managements' objectives in introducing profit-sharing/share-ownership schemes in the company?
b) Do you think these objectives have been met?
   If no, can you recommend any other alternative schemes which would be more likely to achieve these aims?

4 Schemes – specific

Ask same questions for all types of scheme:
SAYE Share Option Schemes

Executive Share Option Schemes
Profit-sharing Schemes

a) Does your union approve of this type of scheme?
b) What are the advantages/disadvantages?
c) Any changes you would like made to this scheme?

5 Employee involvement

a) Are union/management relations in the company satisfactory?
b) Do you think profit-sharing/share-ownership schemes should be on the negotiating agenda?
c) Would you like to see profit sharing/share ownership form part of fixed income/wages/salary?
d) Have the members' attitude to the union changed since the schemes were introduced?
e) How did you hear about the schemes in the company?
f) Was your union consulted about the schemes? Was this satisfactory?
g) How did your members find out about the schemes?
h) Was the information provided satisfactory?
   If not, how could it have been improved?
i) Did your members have any difficulty in understanding the scheme?
   If yes, how could the information/communication be improved?
j) Has financial participation by employees . . .
   i) Improved the efficiency of your members?
   ii) Changed their attitudes towards the union?
   iii) Changed their attitudes to work?
k) Has the introduction of the schemes changed management –union relations in any way?

Profit sharing and share ownership for employees

Employee questionnaire

Profit sharing and share ownership for employees

1 The research into this highly topical issue is sponsored by the Department of Employment. It is concerned with the adoption of profit-sharing and share-ownership schemes following recent legislation. The research is being carried out independently by a research team headed by Professor Michael Poole of the Cardiff Business School, the University College of Wales, Cardiff. *We can thus assure you that the replies you give will be treated in the strictest of confidence.* Indeed, the results will largely be reported in statistical summaries.

2 This questionnaire has been prepared to obtain views on profit-sharing and share-ownership schemes.

3 We realise that you have many demands on your time, so we greatly appreciate your help.

4 Most of the questions ask you to respond to a statement by *circling a number* of the response which you select.

The following is an example of a question.

   1 I enjoy the weather in Britain

Strongly disagree	Disagree	Slightly disagree	Neither agree nor disagree	Slightly agree	Agree	Strongly agree
1	2	3	4	5	6	7

If you *agree* with the statement 'I enjoy the weather in Britain' you would circle number 6. If you *strongly disagree* with the statement, you would circle number 1.

   Some questions do not ask you to agree or disagree, but may ask you how often something happens or whether you think something has *increased* or *decreased* or simply ask for factual information. Other questions are open ended to give you a chance to indicate your views.

5 If you have read a question carefully but still do not fully understand it, just answer it as best you can. We are still interested in receiving your questionnaire even if you are doubtful about one or two questions.

Thank you very much again for your help.

Michael Poole BA (Econ) PhD
Professor
Cardiff Business School
University of Wales Institute of Science and Technology
Cardiff
CF1 3EU

The following question seeks your views on profit-sharing/and share-ownership schemes in general

1 To what extent are you in favour of the development of profit-sharing/share-ownership schemes for employees in British companies?

Please respond to each category

	Strongly in favour	In favour	Neither in favour nor against	Against	Strongly against
(a) Profit sharing (with cash awards)	1	2	3	4	5
(b) Profit sharing (through shares in the company)	1	2	3	4	5
(c) Save As You Earn Share-Ownership Schemes	1	2	3	4	5
(d) Executive Share Schemes	1	2	3	4	5

The next group of questions relate to experiences in your own company

2 As a result of profit sharing/share ownership in your company, do you feel

	Decreased greatly	Decreased considerably	Decreased slightly	Not changed	Increased slightly	Increased considerably	Increased greatly
(a) Your overall satisfaction working for this firm has	1	2	3	4	5	6	7
(b) Your feeling of job security has	1	2	3	4	5	6	7
(c) The amount of effort that you put into your job has.	1	2	3	4	5	6	7

(d) The amount of *productive* work you do has	1	2	3	4	5	6	7
(e) The amount of *effort* other people you work with put into their jobs has	1	2	3	4	5	6	7
(f) In general, employees' say in decisions concerning their own jobs has	1	2	3	4	5	6	7
(g) In general, employees' say in decisions in their own departments has	1	2	3	4	5	6	7
(h) In general, employees' say in overall policies of the firm has	1	2	3	4	5	6	7
(i) *Your* say in decisions concerning your job has	1	2	3	4	5	6	7
(j) *Your* say in decisions in your department has	1	2	3	4	5	6	7
(k) *Your* say in decisions concerning overall policies of the firms has	1	2	3	4	5	6	7
(l) Communication between management and workers has	1	2	3	4	5	6	7

3 How successful do you feel the schemes have been in terms of the following objectives?

	Very successful	Successful	Neither successful nor unsuccessful	Unsuccessful	Not at all successful	Don't know
(a) To make employees more profit conscious/more interested in the company's success	5	4	3	2	1	9
(b) To increase employees' sense of commitment to the company/make staff more likely to stay	5	4	3	2	1	9
(c) To act as an incentive for greater productivity	5	4	3	2	1	9
(d) To make employees feel that they are part of the company – working *with* it, not just *for* it	5	4	3	2	1	9
(e) To help hold down wage claims	5	4	3	2	1	9
(f) To provide a tax efficient means of reward						
for the employees	5	4	3	2	1	9
for the company	5	4	3	2	1	9
(g) To ensure that employees benefit from the company's profitability	5	4	3	2	1	9

(h) To increase employees' understanding of the financial issues that face the company   5   4   3   2   1   9

(i) To increase the sense of cooperation between management and workforce   5   4   3   2   1   9

4 Whom do you feel profit sharing/share ownership benefit the most?

1 Workers   2 Managers   3 Undecided   4 Both equally

5 How did you find out about your company's scheme?

a) Via standard Inland Revenue booklet   1
b) Special company booklet   2
c) Memo   3
d) Video   4
e) Staff meetings   5
f) Via union channels   6
g) Other (*write in*) _____ 7

6 How adequate was this information?

Highly adequate 1	Adequate 2	Neither adequate nor inadequate 3	Inadequate 4	Highly inadequate 5

7 Please specify any improvements you would like to see in communications on profit-sharing or share-ownership schemes in the company

8 How satisfactory do you find your own company's schemes in terms of rewards for employees?

	Highly satisfactory	Satisfactory	Neither satisfactory nor unsatisfactor	Unsatisfactory	Highly unsatisfactory
(a) Profit Sharing (ADST)	1	2	3	4	5
(b) Share Ownership (SAYE)	1	2	3	4	5
(c) Executive Share Option	1	2	3	4	5

9 (a) If you had a choice between a cash-based or a share-based profit-sharing scheme would you choose?

(i)	Cash-based	1
(ii)	Share-based	2
(iii)	Share-based (in a Trust)	3
(iv)	Mixed	4
(v)	Don't know	9

(b) How would you prefer your entitlement to be decided?

(i)	Length of service	1
(ii)	Grade of job	2
(iii)	Salary/wage level	3
(iv)	Flat rate equally	4
(v)	Combination of above	5
(vi)	Don't know	9

For employees in a company with a share-option scheme

10 *Do you participate in the Save As You Earn scheme currently operating in your company?*

Yes 1   No 2

(a) If *yes*
Do you intend to keep your shares?
(i)   for the minimum period necessary   1
(ii)   for the minimum period to qualify for any tax exemption   2
(iii) for 1–2 years after the minimum period   3
(iv)   for period to gain full exemption from income tax   4
(v)   for a substantial period of time   5
(vi)   indefinitely   6

(b) If *no*
Have you ever been part of the Save As You Earn scheme in your company?
Yes 1   No 2

(c) If *yes*, why did you leave it?

The following questions relate to possible improvements or developments in types of scheme

11 *In addition to current arrangements in your company, what other types (if any) of profit-sharing or share-ownership schemes would you like to see developed?*

Please specify

12 *What other types of incentive (if any) do you feel should be introduced to encourage the further spread of profit-sharing and/or share-ownership schemes in companies in Britain?*

Please specify

The following questions ask you to rate how much say or influence there is in each situation below

13 *How much say or influence do you feel that employees in general in this firm actually have in decisions about*

	No say at all	Very little say	Little say	Some say	Good deal of say	Great deal of say	Very great deal of say
(a) Overall policies of the firm	1	2	3	4	5	6	7
(b) Matters affecting their own department	1	2	3	4	5	6	7
(c) How their own jobs are done	1	2	3	4	5	6	7

14 *How much say or influence do you feel that employees in general should have in decisions regarding*

	No say at all	Very little say	Little say	Some say	Good deal of say	Great deal of say	Very great deal of say
(a) Overall policies of the firm	1	2	3	4	5	6	7
(b) Matters affecting their own department	1	2	3	4	5	6	7
(c) How their own jobs are done	1	2	3	4	5	6	7

15 *How much say or influence do you feel you actually have in decisions about*

(a) Overall policies of the firm	1	2	3	4	5	6	7
(b) Matters affecting your own department	1	2	3	4	5	6	7
(c) How your own job is done	1	2	3	4	5	6	7

16 *How much say or influence do you feel you should have in decisions about*

(a) Overall policies of the firm	1	2	3	4	5	6	7
(b) Matters affecting your own department	1	2	3	4	5	6	7
(c) How your own job is done	1	2	3	4	5	6	7

The following questions seek your opinions about unions. Please answer these questions whether or not you are a union member

17

	Strongly disagree	Disagree	Slightly disagree	Neither agree nor disagree	Slightly agree	Agree	Strongly agree
(a) Basically, the union and management have similar goals	1	2	3	4	5	6	7
(b) It is difficult to be loyal to the company *and* to the union	1	2	3	4	5	6	7
(c) A union is not really necessary in this firm at this time	1	2	3	4	5	6	7
(d) There is no reason why the union and management cannot work together	1	2	3	4	5	6	7
(e) Without a union, employees would probably *not* get fair treatment from management	1	2	3	4	5	6	7
(f) The union works primarily for the best interests of its members	1	2	3	4	5	6	7
(g) The best way of obtaining worker say or influence in decision-making in this firm is through increasing the influence of the union	1	2	3	4	5	6	7

The following questions ask you to rate the extent that you feel something

18 At your company to what extent do you

	Little extent		Moderate extent			Very great extent	
(a) Feel a sense of ownership	1	2	3	4	5	6	7
(b) Simply feel like an employee	1	2	3	4	5	6	7
(c) Feel a sense of self employment	1	2	3	4	5	6	7
(d) Feel a sense of pride in working here	1	2	3	4	5	6	7

Please indicate to what extent you agree or disagree with the following statements

19

	Strongly agree				Strongly disagree
(a) The most important element in any job is the pay	1	2	3	4	5
(b) It's important for an employee to feel fully a part of the company	1	2	3	4	5
(c) It's essential for the employee to participate in decision-making	1	2	3	4	5
(d) Work and home should be sharply separated	1	2	3	4	5
(e) The best representative of the employee's interests is the union not the company	1	2	3	4	5
(f) It's important for management and the workforce to trust one another	1	2	3	4	5
(g) A person's own individual career is more important than any loyalty to a particular company	1	2	3	4	5

Information about yourself

The following information is needed to help classify and interpret your previous responses. It will not be used in any way to try to identify individuals. Please answer these questions by circling the number of the correct answer.

20 Are you

1 Male   2 Female

21 At which type of school did you obtain the major part of your secondary education?

(a) Independent   1
(b) State   2
(c) Other   3

22 Do you have any educational/professional qualifications?

1 Yes   2 No

If *yes*, circle as many as apply

(a) CSE, 'O' levels   1
(b) 'A' levels   1
(c) Technical qualifications (*eg* ONC, OND, HNC, HND)   1

Degree

(d) Science   1
(e) Technology   1
(f) Other   1
(g) Higher degree   1
(h) Professional qualifications   1

23 Are you

Married   Single   Widowed   Divorced
1   2   3   4

24 *How many dependents do you have? (Others who depend on you for financial support)*

25 *Do you hold shares*

(a) In this company?   1 Yes   2 No
    If yes
    (i) Did you purchase the shares?   1 Yes   2 No
    (ii) Were you given the shares?   1 Yes   2 No
(b) In another company?   1 Yes   2 No

26 *Do you own or are you in the process of purchasing your home?*

(a) Yes   1
(b) No   2

27 *Are you:*

1 Full-time employee   2 Part-time employee

28 *How many hours do you work in an average week?*

29 *How long have you worked for this company?*

1 Less than six months
2 Six months to eleven months
3 One year or more but less than two years
4 Two to five years
5 Six to ten years
6 Eleven to 15 years
7 More than 15 years

30 *What type of job do you have? (Select only one type)*

1 Senior management
2 Intermediate management
3 Junior management
4 Clerical or secretarial
5 Skilled manual
6 Semi skilled manual
7 Unskilled manual
8 Other: please specify..

31 *How long have you been in your present job in this firm?*

1 Less than one month
2 One to three months
3 More than three to twelve months
4 More than twelve months to three years
5 More than three years to six years
6 More than six years

32 *Are you a member of a staff association*
(a) Yes   1
(b) No   2

33 *Are you a union member?*
1 Yes   2 No
(a) *If yes, are you or have you ever been a steward, or other union officer?*
1 Yes   2 No
(b) *How regularly do you attend main meetings?*

Always	Frequently	Regularly	Occasionally	Never
1	2	3	4	5

34 *What is your age in years?* ....

35 *At the height of their working careers into what category would your father's and your mother's occupation have fallen?*

	Father's	Mother's
(a) Professional or senior managerial (*eg* doctor, company director)	1	1
(b) Semi-professional, middle or lower management (*eg* school teacher, sales manager)	2	2
(c) Routine non-manual (*eg* clerk, typist)	3	3
(d) Skilled manual (*eg* electrician)	4	4
(e) Semi-skilled manual (*eg* machine operative)	5	5
(f) Unskilled manual (*eg* labourer)	6	6
(g) Not in a paid occupation	7	7

36 *What country did your father and mother originally come from?*

	Father	Mother
(a) United Kingdom (England, Scotland, Wales, N. Ireland)	1	1
(b) Eire (Republic of Ireland)	2	2
(c) West Indies/Guyana	3	3
(d) India	4	4
(e) Pakistan	5	5
(f) Bangladesh/East Pakistan	6	6
(g) Africa (Asian origin)	7	7
(h) Africa (other)	8	8
(i) Don't know	9	9
(j) Other: please specify	10	10

37 *For how many other employers have you worked in your working life?*

None	1
One	2
Two	3
Three	4
Four	5
More than four	6

If there is anything you wish to add, particularly on profit-sharing/share-ownership schemes, please feel free to do so in the space below.

Many thanks again for your help.

Appendix five

List of trade unions referred to in the study

AEU	Amalgamated Engineering Union
ASTMS	Association of Scientific, Technical and Managerial Staffs
BIFU	Banking, Insurance and Finance Union
CPSA	Civil and Public Services Association
GMBATU	General, Municipal, Boilermakers and Allied Trade Union
IPCS	Institution of Professional Civil Servants
NALHM	National Association of Licensed House Managers
NUTGW	National Union of Tailors and Garment Workers
TGWU	Transport and General Workers' Union
USDAW	Union of Shop, Distributive and Allied Workers

Note: Names applicable at time of case study investigation.

Bibliography

Acton Society Trust (1959) *Wider Shareholding*, London: Acton Society Trust.

Acton Society Trust and Naylor, G. (1986) *Sharing the Profits: An Inquiry into the Habits, Attitudes and Problems of Employees' Shareholding Schemes*, the text of two studies made for the Wider Share Ownership Council, one by Acton Society Trust and the other by Guy Naylor, London: Garstone Press.

Albrecht, S. (1983) 'Sweden: nationwide debate on worker investment', *Workplace Democracy*, 10, 2, pp. 12–15.

Argyris, C. (1964) *Integrating the Individual and the Organization*, New York: Wiley.

Ashley, W. J. (1913) 'Profit sharing', *Quarterly Review*, CCXIX, pp. 509–30.

Askwith, M. E. (1926) *Profit Sharing, An Aid to Trade Revival: An Exposition of the Case for and Theory of Profit Sharing*, London: Duncan Scott.

Australian Department of Labour and National Service, Industrial Welfare Division (1947) *Profit Sharing: A Study of the Results of Overseas Experience*, Melbourne.

Bader, E. (1971) 'From profit sharing to common ownership', *Journal of Current Social Issues*, 10, 1, pp. 4–15.

Bailey, R. and Ross, B. (1979) 'Profit sharing at the Midland', *Personnel Management*, XI, 3, March, pp. 37–9.

Bell, D. W. (1972) 'Employee savings trust', *Industrial Participation*, DL, Winter, pp. 15–19.

Bell, D. W. (1973a) 'Budget proposals: share savings scheme for all employees', *Industrial Participation*, DLI, Spring, pp. 14–15.

Bell, D. W. (1973b) *Financial Participation: Wages, Profit Sharing and Employee Shareholding*, London: Industrial Participation Association.

Bell, D. W. (1975) *Employee Shareholding Trusts*, London: Industrial Participation Association.

Bell, D. W. (1977a) 'Profit sharing and employee shareholding', *Industrial Participation*, DLXI, pp. 9–12.

Bell, D. W. (1977b) *Profit Sharing, Value Added and Productivity*

Schemes Compared, revised edition, Sept, London: Industrial
Participation Association.

Bell, D. W. (1978) 'Profit sharing and productivity plans: case study',
Industrial Participation, DLXIII, Winter, pp. 3–9.

Bell, D. W. (1979) *Industrial Participation*, London: Pitman.

Bell, D. W. (1980) *Profit Sharing and Employee Shareholding Report*,
London: Industrial Participation Association.

Bell, D. W. and Hanson, C. G. (1984) *Profit Sharing and Employee
Shareholding Attitude Survey*, London: Industrial Participation
Association.

Bell, D. W. and Hanson, C. G. (1987) *Profit Sharing and Profitability*,
London: Kogan Page.

Bellas, C. J. (1972) *Industrial Democracy and the Worker Owned Firm:
A Study of Twenty-one Plywood Companies in the Pacific Northwest*,
New York: Praeger.

Bhagat, S., Brickley, J. and Lease, R. (1985) 'Incentive effects of
stock purchase plans', *Journal of Financial Economics*, 14,
pp. 195–215.

Blanchflower, D. G. and Oswald, A. J. (1987a) 'Profit sharing – can it
work?', *Oxford Economic Papers*, 39, 1, pp. 1–19.

Blanchflower, D. G. and Oswald, A. J. (1987b) 'Shares for employees:
a test of their effects', *Centre for Labour Economics*, Discussion
Paper No 273, October, London School of Economics.

Blum, F. H. (1968) *Work and Community: The Scott Bader
Commonwealth and the Quest for a New Social Order*, London:
Routledge & Kegan Paul.

Board of Trade (1891) *Report of Profit Sharing* (Cd 6267), London:
HMSO.

Board of Trade (1895) *Report on Profit Sharing* (Cd 7458), London:
HMSO.

Board of Trade (1895) *Report on Gain Sharing and Certain Other
Systems of Bonus Production* (Cd 7848), London: HMSO.

Board of Trade (1901) *Report on Profit Sharing and Labour
Co-Partnership Abroad* (Cd 7283), London: HMSO.

Board of Trade (1912) *Report on Profit Sharing and Co-Partnership in
the United Kingdom* (Cd 698), London: HMSO.

Board of Trade (1920) *Report on Profit Sharing and Labour
Co-Partnership in the United Kingdom* (Cd 544), London: HMSO.

Bowie, J. A. (1923) *Sharing the Profits with Employees: A Critical
Study of Methods in the Light of Present Conditions*, Second
Edition, London: Pitman.

Bradley, K. (1986) 'Employee ownership and economic decline in
western industrialized democracies', *Journal of Management Studies*,
23, 2, pp. 51–71.

Bradley, K. and Gelb, A. (1983a) *Co-operation at Work: The
Mondragon Experience*, London: Heinemann.

Bradley, K. and Gelb, A. (1983b) *Worker Capitalism: The New
Industrial Relations*, London: Heinemann.

Brannen, P. (1983) *Authority and Participation in Industry*, London: Batsford.

Brannen, P., Batstone, E., Fatchett, D. and White, P. (1976) *The Worker Directors*, London: Hutchinson.

Brassey, T. (1898) *Co-operative and Profit Sharing Industries, With Remarks on Trade Unions*, Melbourne: Echo Publishing.

Breakwell, B. (1980) 'Profit-sharing schemes under the new rules', *Accountancy*, July, pp. 107–9.

Breakwell, B. (1983) 'Profit-sharing and the Finance Acts 1978 to 1983: A case for a review of incentives', *Accounting and Business Research*, Winter, pp. 3–14.

Bristow, E. (1974) 'Profit sharing, socialism and labour unrest', in Brown, K. D. (ed.), *Essays in Anti-Labour History*, London: Macmillan.

British Institute of Management (1974) *Share Incentive Schemes for Executives: A Survey of Current Practice*, London: BIM.

BJIR Chronicle (1978a) 'Government policy and activities: profit-sharing schemes', *British Journal of Industrial Relations*, 16, 3, Nov, pp. 3 and 381.

BJIR Chronicle (1978b) 'The employees: profit-sharing schemes', *British Journal of Industrial Relations*, 16, 3, Nov, pp. 3 and 386.

Brolly, M. H. (1960) 'Profit sharing', *Occupational Psychology*, 34, 2, pp. 86–108.

Brooks, L., Henry, J. and Livingstone, D. (1982) 'How profitable are employee stock ownership plans?' *Financial Executive*, May.

Brown, W. (1981) *The Changing Contours of British Industrial Relations*, Oxford: Basil Blackwell.

Burton, G. (1982) 'Employee share schemes – the way ahead?' *Accountancy*, Nov, pp. 62–4.

Burton, J. F. (Jr) (ed.) (1986) Review Symposium, 'The share economy: Conquering stagflation', by M. Weitzman, *Industrial and Labor Relations Review*, 39, 2, Jan, pp. 285–90.

Bushill, T. W. (1983) *Profit Sharing and the Labour Question*, London: Methuen.

Button, H. (1918) *Notes on the Principles of Profit Sharing and Labour Co-partnership*, London: Boyle & Watchurst.

Cable, J. and Fitzroy, F. R. (1980) 'Production efficiency, incentives and employee participation: some preliminary results from West Germany', *Kyklos*, 33, pp. 100–21.

Carpenter, C. C. (1912) *Co-Partnership in Industry*, London: Co-Partnership Publications.

Cavaghan, R. L. (1973) 'Employee attitudes to profit sharing: a research report', *Industrial Participation*, DLIII, Autumn-Winter, pp. 15–18.

Cecil, R. and Clynes, J. R. (1919) *Speeches on Profit-Sharing and Labour Co-Partnership*, London: Co-Partnership Publications.

Christiansen, R. O. (1980) 'Impact of employee stock ownership plans on employee morale', *American Journal of Small Business*, 5, 1, July–Sept, pp. 22–9.

Church, R. A. (1971) 'Profit sharing and labour relations in England in the nineteenth century', *International Review of Social History*, XVI, 1, pp. 2–16.

Cole, G. D. H. (1957) *The Case for Industrial Partnership*, London: Macmillan.

Confederation of British Industry (1978) *Financial Participation in Companies: An Introductory Booklet*, London: CBI.

Conservative Research Department (1946) *Co-partnership today: A survey of profit sharing and co-partnership schemes in industry* (second edition, 1955), London: Conservative Political Centre.

Conte, M. and Tannenbaum, A. S. (1978) 'Employee owned companies: Is the difference measurable?' *Monthly Labor Review*, 101, pp. 23–8.

Conte, M., Tannenbaum, A. S. and McCullough, A. F. (1980) *Employee Ownership*, Ann Arbor, MI: Institute of Survey Research.

Cooke, H. E. T. (1919) *How Capital and Labour Can Share Equally in Net Profits?* Montreal: published by the author.

Copeman, G. H. (1958) *The Challenge of Employee Shareholding: How to Close the Gap Between Capital and Labour*, London: Batsford.

Copeman, G. H. (1974) *Employee Participation in Nationalized and Other Enterprises*, London: Aims of Industry.

Copeman, G. H. (1975) *Employee Share Ownership and Industrial Stability*, London: Institute of Personnel Management.

Copeman, G. H. (1976) 'Employee participation in capital growth', *Management Decisions*, XIV, 2, pp. 71–102.

Copeman, G. H. (1977) 'Share and reward schemes', *Personnel Management*, IX, 1, Jan, pp. 34–7.

Copeman, G. H. (1978) 'Sharing profits by incentives', *Management Today*, Aug, pp. 55–7.

Copeman, G. H. (1979) 'Profit sharing in perspective', *Personnel Management*, XI, 1, Jan, pp. 36–8.

Copeman, G. H. (1980) 'The productivity key', *Management Today*, April, pp. 45–9.

Copeman, G. H. and Moore, P. (1982) 'A new look at the pay round', *Accountancy*, Dec, pp. 125–8.

Copeman, G. H. and Rumble, T. (1972) *Capital as an Incentive*, London: Leviathan House.

Copeman, G. H., Moore, P. and Arrowsmith, C. (1984) *Share Ownership: How to use Capital Incentives to Sustain Business Growth*, Aldershot: Gower.

Creigh, S., Donaldson, N. and Haworth, E. (1981) 'A stake in the firm: employee financial involvement in Britain', *Employment Gazette*, May, pp. 229–36.

Crockatt, J. L. (1977–8) 'Employee shareholding in the Johnson Group: case study', *Industrial Participation*, DLXIII, Winter, pp. 30–6.

Crockatt, J. L. and Nightingale, N. J. (1977–8) 'Employee shareholding case histories', *Industrial Participation*, DLXIII, Winter, pp. 30–42.

Crossley, J. R. (1969) 'Incomes policy and sharing in capital gains', *British Journal of Industrial Relations*, 7, 3, Nov, pp. 336–52.

Crouch, C. (1982) *Trade Unions: The Logic of Collective Action*, London: Fontana.

Dalal, K. L. (1950) 'Profit-sharing: the experience of foreign countries', *Indian Journal of Economics*, XXXI, 1, July, pp. 1–15.

Daly, G. F. A. (1969) 'Is there a case for profit sharing?' *Industrial Democracy: A Symposium*, Dublin: Irish Management Insitute.

Daniel, W. and Millward, N. (1983) *Workplace Industrial Relations in Britain*, London: Heinemann.

Daw, J. W. (1955) 'Profit sharing and Co-partnership', *The Director*, 2, July-Oct.

Department of Employment (1986) 'Profit related pay: a consultative document', Cd 9835, London: HMSO.

Derrick, P. (1963) 'Is co-ownership the answer?', *New Society*, 31, 2 May, pp. 11–13.

Derrick, P. and Phipps, J. F. (eds) (1969) *Co-Ownership, Co-operation and Control*, London: Longmans.

Dodwell, D. W. (1985) 'Progress with profit sharing', *Contemporary Review*, 187, May, pp. 322–5.

Edwards, P. K. (1987) *Managing the Factory*, Oxford: Basil Blackwell.

Elliott, J. (1978) *Conflict and Co-operation: The Growth of Industrial Democracy*, London: Kogan Page.

ESOP Association (1982) *ESOP Survey, 1982*, Washington DC: The ESOP Association.

Estrin, S. (1978) *An Explanation of Earnings' Variation in the Yugoslav Self-Managed Economy*, Discussion Paper on Economics and Econometrics No 7804, Oct, University of Southampton.

Estrin, S. (1983) *Self-Management: Economic Theory and Yugoslav Practice*, London: Cambridge University Press.

Estrin, S. (1983) *Market Imperfections, Labour Management and Earnings Differentials in a Developing Country: Theory and Evidence from Yugoslavia*, Discussion Paper on Economics and Econometrics No 8317, University of Southampton.

Estrin, S., Grout, P. A. and Wadhwani, S. (1987) 'Profit sharing and employee share ownership', *Economic Policy*, 4, pp. 13–51.

Estrin, S. and Wilson, N. (1986) 'The micro-economic effects of profit-sharing: the British experience', *Centre for Labour Economics*, Discussion Paper No 247, London School of Economics.

Farrow, N. (1965) *The Profit in Worker Ownership*, London: Business Publications.

Farrow, N. (1969a) 'The John Lewis Partnership'. The profit in worker ownership', in Derrick, P. and Phipps, J. F. (eds), *Co-ownership, Co-operation and Control*, London: Longmans.

Farrow, N. (1969b) 'The Scott Bader Commonwealth Ltd', in Derrick, P. and Phipps, J. F. (eds), *Co-ownership, Co-operation and Control*, London: Longmans.

Fitzroy, F. R. and Kraft, K. (1986) 'Profitability and profit sharing', *Journal of Industrial Economics*, 35, pp. 113–30.

Fitzroy, F. R. and Kraft, K. (1987) 'Cooperation, productivity and profit sharing', *Quarterly Journal of Economics*, 11, pp. 23–5.

Flanders, A., Pomeranz, R. and Woodward, J. (1968) *Experiment in Industrial Democracy: A Study of the John Lewis Partnership*, London: Faber.

Flint, D. (1955) 'Profit sharing (benefits, problems of finance and function of industry)', *Accounts Magazine*, 59, July, 1955, pp. 412–32. (Also Aug, pp. 478–96).

Fogarty, M. and White, M. (1988) *Share Schemes as Workers See Them*, London: Policy Studies Institute.

Fox, A. (1985) *History and Heritage: The Social Origins of the British Industrial Relations System*, London: George, Allen & Unwin.

Franklin, J. (1977) 'Company-wide savings related share schemes', *Industrial Participation*, DLX, Winter, pp. 20–2.

Franklin, J. (1977–8), 'Introducing employee shareholding', *Industrial Participation*, DLXIII, Winter, pp. 25–9.

French, J. L. (1987) 'Employee perspectives on stock ownership: financial investment or mechanism of control?', *Academy of Management Journal*, 12, 3, pp. 427–35.

French, J. L. and Rosenstein, J. (1984), 'Employee ownership, work attitudes and power relationships', *Academy of Management Journal*, 27, pp. 861–9.

Garson, G. D. (1975) 'Recent development in workers' participation in Europe', in Vanek, J. (ed.), *Self-Management: Economic Liberation of Man*, Harmondsworth: Penguin, pp. 161–86.

Gilchrist, R. N. (1924) *The Payment of Wages and Profit-Sharing*, Calcutta: University of Calcutta.

Gilman, N. P. (1869) *Profit Sharing Between Employer and Employee*, (reprinted 1971), New York: Books for Libraries Press.

Goddard, H. A. (1939) 'Profit-sharing and the amenities of the Nuffield factories', in Gannett, F. E. and Catherwood, B. F. (eds), *Industrial and Labour Relations in Britain: A symposium*, New York: The Editors, Industrial Co-Partnership Association.

Goldstein, S. (1978) 'Employee share ownership and motivation', *Journal of Industrial Relations*, XX, Sept, pp. 311–30.

Granrose, G. S. (1986) 'Employee ownership and older workers', *Human Relations*, 39, 6, June, pp. 557–76.

Greenberg, E. S. (1980) 'Participation in industrial decision-making and worker satisfaction: the case of producer cooperatives', *Social Science Quarterly*, 60, pp. 551–69.

Greenberg, E. S. (1984) 'Producers' cooperatives and democratic theory: the case of the plywood firms', in Jackall, R. and Levin, H. M. *Worker Cooperatives in America*, Berkeley: University of California Press.

Greenhill, R. (1980) *Employee Remuneration and Profit Sharing*, Cambridge: Woodhead-Faulkner.

Greening, E. O. (1885) 'Profit-sharing and co-operative production',

Industrial Remuneration Conference, *The Report of Proceedings and Papers*, London: Cassell, pp. 304–11.

Grout, P. A. (1987) 'The wider share ownership programme', *Fiscal Studies*, 8, 3, August, pp. 59–74.

Gurdon, M. A. (1985) 'Equity participation by employees: the growing debate in West Germany', *Industrial Relations*, 24, 1, Winter, pp. 113–38.

Hammer, T. H. and Stern, R. N. (1980) 'Employee ownership: Implications for the organizational distribution of power', *Academy of Management Journal*, XXIII, March, pp. 78–100.

Hammer, T. H., Landau, J. C. and Stern, R. N. (1981) 'Absenteeism when workers have a voice: the case of employee ownership', *Journal of Applied Psychology*, 66, 5, pp. 561–71.

Hammer, T. H., Stern, R. N. and Gurdon, M. A. (1982) 'Workers' ownership and attitudes towards participation', in Lindenfeld, F. and Rothschild-Whitt, J. (eds), *Workplace Democracy and Social Change*, Boston: Porter Sargent.

Hanson, C. G. (1965) 'Profit sharing schemes in Great Britain', *Journal of Management Studies*, II, 3, Oct, pp. 331–50.

Hanson, C. G. (1986) 'Employee profit sharing: Weitzmania and wild-goose chases', *Economic Affairs*, Dec, pp. 10–15.

Harper, J. C. (1955) *Profit Sharing in Practice and Law*, London: Sweet & Maxwell.

Harris, N. (1972) *Competition and the Corporate State*, London: Methuen.

Hatton, T. J. (1986) 'Profit sharing in British industry, 1865–1913', *Mimeo*, Department of Economics, University of Essex.

Hazell, W. H. (1962) 'Profit sharing and share purchase for employees', *Quarterly Review*, CCXLVI, Jan, pp. 49–59.

HMSO (1970) *Reports from select committees and other reports on wages, government contracts and on profit sharing, with proceedings, minutes of evidence, appendices and indices, 1890–97*, Shannon: Irish University Press.

Herzberg, F., Mausner, B. and Snyderman, B. (1967) *The Motivation to Work*, second edition, London: Wiley.

Hespe, G. and Wall, T. (1976) 'The demand for participation among employees', *Human Relations*, 29, pp. 411–28.

Hochner, A. and Granrose, C. S. (1983) 'Motivation to choose employee ownership as an alternative to job loss', paper presented at the Annual Meetings of the American Academy of Management.

Incomes Data Services (1974) *Savings Related Share Schemes*, Parts 1 and 2, Studies 70 and 7, London: IDS.

Incomes Data Services (1978a) *Profits Sharing Part 1*, Study 1960, December, London: IDS.

Incomes Data Services (1978b) *Profit Sharing Part 2*, Study 163, February, London: IDS.

Incomes Data Services (1979) *Profit Sharing Schemes*, Study 204, October, London: IDS.

Incomes Data Services (1984) *Profit Sharing and Share Options*, Study 306, Jan, London: IDS.

Incomes Data Services (1985) *Executive Share Options*, IDS Top Pay Unit, Jan, London: IDS.

Incomes Data Services (1986) *Profit Sharing and Share Options*, Study 357, March, London: IDS.

Industrial Relations Review and Report (1975) *Sharing the Profits: A Survey of Company Practice*, 114, Oct, pp. 2–10.

Industrial Relations Review and Report (1978) *Employee Shareholding Trusts*, 189, Dec, pp. 2–6.

Institute of Cost and Works Accountants (1954) *Employee Renumeration and Incentives*, London: ICWA.

International Labour Office (1921) 'Profit-sharing and labour co-partnership in Great Britain', *International Labour Review*, IV, Oct, pp. 114–26.

International Labour Office (1964a) *Bibliography on Cooperation*, revised edition, Geneva: ILO.

International Labour Office (1964b) 'Profit-sharing and co-partnership', in *Wages: A Workers' Educational Manual*, 9th Lesson, Geneva: ILO, pp. 52–8.

Ireland, N. (1987) 'Profit-sharing to promote employment', *Economic Review*, 4, 5, pp. 35–8.

Jehring, J. J. (1954) *A Comprehensive Bibliography of Domestic and Foreign Books and Articles on Profit Sharing*, Evanston, Ill: Profit Sharing Research Foundation.

Jehring, J. J. (1956) *Succeeding with Profit Sharing*, Evanston, Ill: Profit Sharing Research Foundation.

Jehring, J. J. (1968) 'Profit sharing', in Roberts, B. C. *Industrial Relations: Contemporary Issues*, London: Macmillan.

Jenkins, R. (1979) *A General Look At and a Research Project on Employee Ownership*, unpublished report quoted in Sockell, D. (1985), 'Attitudes, behavior and employee ownership: some preliminary data', *Industrial Relations*, 24, 1, pp. 130–8.

Job Ownership Limited (1985) *Employee Ownership – Why? How?*, London: Network Services.

John Lewis Partnership (1969) 'The John Lewis Partnership 2. The partnership system and how it works', in Derrick, P. and Phipps, J. F. (eds), *Co-ownership, Co-operation and Control*, London: Longmans.

Jordan, H. W. (1920) *A National Scheme of Profit Sharing*, London: Industrial League and Council.

Jones, B. (1892) 'Co-operation and profit sharing', *Economic Journal*, II, 8, Dec, pp. 616–28.

Jones, D. C. and Svejnar, J. (eds) (1982) *Participatory and Self-managed Firms: Evaluating Economic Performance*, Lexington, Mass: Lexington Books.

Jones, D. C. and Svejnar, J. (1985) 'Participation, profit sharing, worker ownership and efficiency in Italian producer cooperatives', *Economica*, 52, pp. 449–65.

Jones, T. (1904) *Profit Sharing in Relation to Other Methods of Remuneration Labour*, Edinburgh: Blackwood.

Kelso, L. O. and Adler, M. J. (1958) *The Capitalist Manifesto*, Westport, CT: Greenwood Press.

Kenny, G. K. (1985) 'The beneficiaries of employee ownership: managers or non-managers?', *Journal of General Management*, 11, 2, Winter, pp. 62–73.

Kerr, C., Dunlop, J. T., Harbison, F. H. and Myers, C. A. (1960) *Industrialism and Industrial Man: The Problems of Labor and Management in Economic Growth*, Cambridge, Mass: Harvard University Press.

Keynes, J. M. (1940) *How to Pay for the War*.

Kinley, D. (1891) 'Recent progress of profit sharing abroad', *Quarterly Journal of Economics*, V, July, pp. 497–503.

Klein, K. and Rosen, C. (1986) 'Employee stock ownership in the United States', in Stern, R. N. and McCarthy, S. *International Yearbook of Organizational Democracy*, III, Chichester: Wiley.

Kruse, D. (1984) *Employee Ownership and Employee Attitudes: Two Case Studies*, Penn: Norwood Editions.

Labour Co-partnership Association (1919) *Experiments in Profit Sharing and Co-partnership*, Birmingham: LCA.

Landon, M. (1985) *Employee Share Schemes: How they Operate in 138 Companies*, London: Copeman Paterson.

Lata, G. (1979) *Profit Sharing, Employee Stock Ownership, Savings and Asset Formation in the Western World*: University of Pennsylvania.

Lesieur, F. G. (ed.) (1958) *The Scanlon Plan*, MIT, Mass: The Technology Press.

Lever, W. H. (1901) 'Prosperity-sharing: a rejoinder', *Economic Review*, XI, 3, July, pp. 316–21.

Lewis, J. S. (1948) *Partnership for All*, second edition, 1952, London: Kerr-Cross.

Livesey, G. (1904) 'Industrial partnership and the prevention of distress', in Loch, C. S. (ed.) *Methods and Social Advance: Short Studies in Social Practice by Various Authors*, London: Macmillan, pp. 107–17.

Livingstone, D. and Henry, J. (1980) 'The effect of employee stock ownership plans on corporate profits', *Journal of Risk and Assurance*, 47, pp. 491–505.

Lloyd, P. A. (1976) *Incentive Payment Schemes*, Management Survey Report No 34, London: British Institute of Management.

Long, R. J. (1978a) 'The effects of employee ownership on organizational identification, job attitudes and organizational performance: a tentative framework and empirical findings', *Human Relations*, 31, 1, pp. 29–48.

Long, R. J. (1978b) 'The relative effects of share ownership *vs* control on job attitudes in an employee owned company', *Human Relations*, 31, 9, pp. 753–63.

Long, R. J. (1979) 'Desires for and patterns of worker participation in decision-making after conversion to employee ownership', *Academy of Management Journal*, 22, 3, pp. 611–17.

Long, R. J. (1980a) 'Employee ownership and attitudes toward the union', *Relations Industrielles*, XXXIII, pp. 237–53.

Long, R. J. (1980b) 'Job attitudes and organizational performance under employee ownership', *Academy of Management Journal*, 23, 4, pp. 726–37.

Long, R. J. (1981) 'The effects of formal employee participation in ownership and decision-making on perceived and desired patterns of organizational performance: A longitudinal study', *Human Relations*, 34, 10, pp. 847–76.

Long, R. J. (1982) 'Worker ownership and job attitudes: a field study', *Industrial Relations*, 21, 2, pp. 196–215.

Mackmurdo, A. (1913) *Pressing Questions: Profit Sharing, Women's Suffrage, Electoral Reform*, London: J. Lane.

Majerus, R. E. (1984) 'Workers have a right to a share of the profits', *Harvard Business Review*, Sept/Oct, pp. 42, 44 and 50.

Manchester Guardian Commercial Handbooks (1922) *Practical Profit Sharing: A Survey of Existing Schemes*, Manchester.

Marsh, T. and McAllister, D. (1981) 'ESOPs tables: a survey of companies with employee stock ownership plans', *Journal of Corporation Law*, 6, 3, pp. 557–623.

Masson, R. T. (1971) 'Executive motivations, earnings and consequent equity performance', *Journal of Political Economy*, 79, pp. 1278–92.

Mathieson, G. (1902) 'Some aspects of profit sharing', *Economic Review*, XII, 1, Jan, pp. 35–42.

Meade, J. E. (1964) *Efficiency, Equality and the Ownership of Property*, London: Allen & Unwin.

Meade, J. E. (1972) 'The theory of labour-managed firms and profit sharing', *Economic Journal*, LXXXI, pp. 402–28.

Meade, J. E. (1986) *Different Forms of Share Economy*, London: Public Policy Centre.

Meidner, R. (1978) *Employee Investment Funds*, London: Allen & Unwin.

Meidner, R. (1981) 'Collective asset formation through wage-earner funds', *International Labour Review*, 120, 3, May/June, pp. 303–17.

Melling, J. (1983) 'Employers, industrial welfare and the struggle for workplace control in British industry, 1880–1920', in Gospel H. F. and Littler, C. R. (eds), *Managerial Strategies and Industrial Relations: An Historical and Comparative Study*, London: Heinemann.

Metzger, B. L. (1968) *Profit Sharing: One of the 'New Breed' of Total Systems Incentives*, Evanston, Ill: Profit Sharing Research Foundation.

Metzger, B. L. (1975a) *Pension, Profit Sharing or Both*, Evanston, Ill: Profit Sharing Research Foundation.

Metzger, B. L. (1975b) *Profit Sharing in 38 Large Companies: Volume I*, Evanston, Ill: Profit Sharing Research Foundation.

Metzger, B. L. and Colletti, J. A. (1971) *Does Profit Sharing Pay?* Evanston, Ill: Profit Sharing Research Foundation.

Middleton, M. W. (1903) 'Profit sharing experiments', *Economic Review*, XIII, 2, April, pp. 213–15.

Miller, B. (1976) 'Partnership not participation', *Industrial Participation*, DLIX, Spring, pp. 12–21.

Ministry of Labour (1930) 'Profit sharing and co-partnership in 1929', *Ministry of Labour Gazette*, Vol XXXVIII, 7, July, pp. 238–40.

Mitchell, D. J. B. (1987) 'The share economy and industrial relations', *Industrial Relations*, 26, 1, pp. 1–17.

Monroe, P. 'Profit sharing and cooperation', *American Journal of Sociology*, IV, 5, March, 1899, pp. 593–602; 6, May, 1899, pp. 788–806. Part 1 Theory, Part 2 Great Britain etc.

Morse, G. and William, D. (1979) *Profit Sharing: Legal Aspects of Employee Share Schemes*, London: Sweet & Maxwell.

Mundy, E. W. (1931) *Profit-Sharing and Co-Partnership: An Introduction*, third edition, London: Labour Co-Partnership Association.

Murray, I. (1973) *Workers' Shares and Savings*, London: Working Together Campaign.

Myrdal, H. (1981) 'Collective wage-earner funds in Sweden: a road to socialism and the end of freedom of association', *International Labour Review*, 120, May/June, pp. 319–34.

Narasimhan, P. S. (1960) 'Profit sharing: a review', *International Labour Review*, 99, Dec, pp. 469–99.

National Civic Federation, Profit Sharing Department (1921) *Profit Sharing by American Employees, Examples from England, Types in France*, New York: NCF.

National Union of Bank Employees (1975) *Profit Sharing and Stock Options in Britain and Europe*, Twickenham: NUBE.

National Union of Conservative and Constitutional Associations, Advisory Committee on Policy and Political Education (1946) *Co-Partnership Today: A Survey of Profit-Sharing and Co-Partnership Schemes in Industry*, London.

Nichols, T. (1964) *Ownership, Control and Ideology*, London: Allen & Unwin.

Nicholson, J. S. (1896) 'Profit sharing', in *Strikes and Social Problems*, London: Black, pp. 45–69.

Nightingale, N. J. (1977–8) 'Employee share option schemes in Rowntree Mackintosh Ltd: case study', *Industrial Participation*, DLXIII, Winter, pp. 37–43.

Nuti, D. M. (1987) 'Profit sharing and employment: claims and overclaims', *Industrial Relations*, 26, 1, Winter, pp. 18–29.

Oliver, N. (1984) 'An examination of organizational commitment in six worker cooperatives in Scotland', *Human Relations*, 37, Jan, pp. 29–45.

PA Services (1985–6) 'What is happening in the world?' *Industrial Participation*, 589, Winter, pp. 17–25.

Patard, R. J. (1982) 'Employee stock ownership in the 1920s', *Employee Ownership*, 2, 3, Sept, pp. 4–5.

Pease, E. R. (1921) *Profit Sharing and Co-Partnership*, London: Labour Party.

Phillips, L. (1900) 'Two profit sharing concerns', *Economic Review*, X, 2, April, pp. 239–41.

Pierce, J. L., Rubenfeld, S. A. and Morgan, S. (1988) *Employee Ownership: A Conceptual Model of Process and Effects*, Duluth: University of Minnesota, Department of Management Studies.

Pollard, S. and Turner, R. (1976) 'Profit sharing and autocracy', *Business History*, XVIII, 1, January, pp. 4–34.

Poole, M. J. F. (1986) *Towards a New Industrial Democracy: Workers Participation in Industry*, London: Routledge & Kegan Paul.

Poole, M. J. F. (1988) 'Factors affecting the development of employee financial participation in contemporary Britain', *British Journal of Industrial Relations*, 26, 1, pp. 21–36.

Poole, M. J. F. (1989) *The Origins of Economic Democracy*, London: Routledge.

Powell, A. (1887) 'Profit sharing, historically and theoretically considered', *Journal of the American Social Science Association*, 23, Nov, pp. 48–67.

Price, L. F. R. (1892) 'Profit sharing and co-operative production', *Economic Journal*, II, 7, Sept, pp. 442–62.

Purcell, J. and Sisson, K. (1983) 'Strategies and practice in the management of industrial relations', in Bain, G. S. (ed.), *Industrial Relations in Britain*, Oxford: Basil Blackwell, pp. 95–120.

Quarterly Review (1905) 'Profit-sharing and co-partnership', *Quarterly Review*, CCIII, 402, pp. 61–87.

Ramage, J. (1939) 'Profit-sharing and co-partnership in Great Britain', in Gannett, F. E. and Catherwood, B. F. (eds), *Industrial and Labour Relations in Great Britain: A Symposium*, New York: The Editors, Industrial Co-Partnership Association.

Ramsay, H. (1978) 'Cycles of control: worker participation in sociological and historical perspective', *Sociology*, 11, pp. 481–506.

Ramsay, H. (1983) 'Evolution or cycle? Worker participation in the 1970s and 1980s', in Crouch, C. and Heller, F. A. (eds), *International Yearbook of Organizational Democracy*, I, Chichester: Wiley, pp. 203–25.

Ramsay, H. and Haworth, N. (1984) 'Worker capitalists? Profit sharing, capital sharing and juridical forms of socialism', *Economic and Industrial Democracy*, 5, 3, pp. 295–324.

Ramsay, H., Leopold, J. and Hyman, J. (1986) 'Profit-sharing and employee share-ownership: an initial assessment', *Employee Relations*, 8, 1, pp. 23–6.

Rawson, H. G. (1891) *Profit Sharing Precedents, with Notes*, London: Stevens.

Reilly, P. A. (1978) *Employee Financial Participation*, London: British Institute of Management.

Remus, J. (1983) 'Financial participation of employees: an attempted classification and major trends', *International Labour Review*, 122, 1, January/February, pp. 1−20.

Reynolds, M. (1973) 'Ownership in work', *Management Education and Development*, 4, 2, pp. 86−94.

Rhodes, S. R. and Steers, R. M. (1981) 'Conventional *vs* worker-owned firms', *Human Relations*, 34, pp. 1013−35.

Richardson, R. and Nejad, A. (1986) 'Employee share ownership schemes in the UK: an evaluation', *British Journal of Industrial Relations*, 24, 2, pp. 233−50.

Rogow, A. (1955) 'Labour relations under the British Labour Government: profit sharing and co-partnership', *American Journal of Sociology*, 14, July, pp. 371−4.

Rosen, C. and Klein, K. J. (1983) 'Job-creating performance of employee-owned firms', *Monthly Labor Review*, 106, 8, pp. 15−19.

Rosen, C., Klein, K. J. and Young, K. M. (1985) *Employee Ownership in America: The Equity Solution*, Lexington: Heath.

Roskin, A. H. (1968) 'Profit sharing in the pay check: cure for the wage price spiral?', *Saturday Review*, 51, 10 February, pp. 21−4, 48.

Rothschild-Whitt, J. and Whitt, J. A. (1986) 'Worker-owners as an emergent class: effects of co-operative work on job satisfaction, alienation and stress', *Economic and Industrial Democracy*, 7, pp. 297−317.

Rowntree, S. (1982) 'Profit sharing in industry', *Industrial Society*, June.

Royal Commission on Labour (1892−4), Cd 6709, London: Her Majesty's Stationery Office.

Royal Commission on Trade Unions (1867−9) Cd 4132, London: Her Majesty's Stationery Office.

Russell, R. (1984) 'Using ownership to control: making workers owners in the contemporary United States', *Politics and Society*, 13, 3, pp. 253−94.

Russell, R. (1985) *Sharing Ownership in the Workplace*, Albany, NY: State University of New York Press.

Russell, R., Hochner, A. and Perry, S. E. (1979) 'Participation, influence and worker ownership', *Industrial Relations*, 18, 3, pp. 330−41.

Schloss, D. F. (1890) 'Profit-sharing', *Charity Organization Review*, VI, January, pp. 10−16.

Schloss, D. F. (1891) 'The increase in industrial remuneration under profit sharing', *Economic Journal*, 1, 2, June, pp. 292−303.

Schroeder, E. A., Sherman, J. D. and Elmore, R. C. (1987) 'A long-term profit-sharing plan to stimulate motivation and innovation among R&D personnel', *Personnel Review*, 16, 3, pp. 34−8.

Smith, G. R. (1986) 'Profit sharing and employee share ownership in Britain', *Employment Gazette*, Sept, pp. 380−5.

Smith, J. C. (1908) *Money and Profit Sharing*, London: Paul, Trench & Trubner.

Smith, J. C. (1913) 'The theory of equitable profit-sharing', *Westminster Review*, CLXXX, 5, Nov, pp. 492–512.

Smith, J. H. (1945) 'Some consideration affecting the operation of profit-sharing schemes in farming', in *Welsh Studies in Agricultural Economics*: University College of Wales, Aberystwyth, Department of Agricultural Economics.

Snell, W. E. (1893) 'Co-operators and profit sharing', *Economic Review*, III, 2, April, pp. 201–11.

Sockell, D. (1983) 'Toward a theory of the union's role in an enterprise', in Lipsky, D. B. and Douglas, J. M. (eds), *Advances in Industrial and Labor Relations: A Research Annual*, I, Connecticut: Jai Press Inc, pp. 221–82.

Sockell, D. (1985) 'Attitudes, behavior and employee ownership: some preliminary data', *Industrial Relations*, 24, 1, pp. 130–8.

Steinherr, A. (1977) 'On the efficiency of profit sharing and labor participation in management', *Bell Journal of Economics*, 8, 2, Autumn.

Stern, R. N. and O'Brien, R. A. (1977) 'National unions and employee ownership', *Mimeo*, Cornell University.

Stern, R. N. and Hammer, T. H. (1978) 'Buying your job: factors affecting the success or failure of employee acquisition attempts', *Human Relations*, 31, pp. 1101–17.

Stern, R. N., Whyte, W. F., Hammer, T. H. and Meek, C. B. (1983) 'The union and the transition to employee ownership', in Whyte, W. F., Hammer, T. H., Meek, C. B., Nelson, R. and Stern, R. N. *Worker Participation and Ownership*, Ithaca, NY: ILR Press, Cornell University.

Stock Exchange (1986) 'The changing face of share ownership', London: Stock Exchange.

Stocks, J. L. (1912) 'Profit sharing in operation', *Economic Review*, XXII, 3, pp. 313–17.

Strauss, G. (1986) 'Participation and Gainsharing', *Mimeo*, University of California, Berkeley.

Taylor, H. E. (1956) 'Pension and profit sharing plans', *Mississippi Law Journal*, 28, Dec, pp. 1–19.

Tannenbaum, A. S. (1983) 'Employee owned companies', in Cummings, L. L. and Staw, B. M. (eds), *Research in Organizational Behaviour*, 5, Greenwich, CT: JAI Press.

Tannenbaum, A. S., Cooke, H. and Lohmann, J. (1984) *A Research Report: The Relationship of Employee Ownership to the Technological Adaptiveness and Performance of Companies*, January, Ann Arbor, MI: Institute for Survey Research, University of Michigan.

Taylor, J. (1983) 'Scott Bader: A common ownership response to crisis', MSc Thesis: Industrial Relations and Personnel Department, London School of Economics.

Taylor, S. (1882–3) 'On profit sharing between capital and labour', *Manchester Statistical Society Transcript*, pp. 65–92.

Taylor, S. (1884) *Profit Sharing between Capital and Labour*, London: Kegan Paul, Trench & Co.

Taylor, T. C. (1912) 'Profit sharing and labour co-partnership', *Contemporary Review*, CL, May, pp. 625–34.

Thomason, G. F. (1973) 'Workers' participation in private enterprise organizations', in Balfour, C. (ed.), *Participation in Industry*, London: Croom Helm, pp. 138–80.

The Times (1986) 'Profit sharing bogged down in caution', 13 May.

Toscano, D. J. (1983) 'Towards a typology of employee ownership', *Human Relations*, 36, July, pp. 581–601.

Trombert, A. (1920) *Profit Sharing: A General Study of the Systems as in Actual Operation*, London: P. S. King and Son.

Turner, G. (1969) *Business in Britain*, London: Eyre & Spottiswoode.

Vinson, N. (1973) 'Participation in Profit', *Industrial Society*, LV, 8, August, pp. 14–17.

Vroom, V. (1964) *Work and Motivation*, New York: John Wiley.

Wagner, I. (1984) Report to the New York Stock Exchange on the performance of publicly held employee ownership companies. Unpublished manuscript, Arlington, VA, National Center for Employee Ownership.

Wainwright, R. (1958) *Own as you Earn*, London: Liberal Publications Department.

Wallace, W. (1966) 'Profit sharing schemes in Great Britain: a comment', *Journal of Management Studies*, III, 1, February, pp. 122–3.

Webb, S. and Webb, B. (1897) *Industrial Democracy*, London: Longmans, Green.

Webb, S. and Webb, B. (1902) *A History of Trade Unionism*, London: Longmans, Green.

Webb, S. and Webb, B. (1914) 'Co-operative production and profit sharing', *New Statesman*, 45, 14 Feb, supplement.

Weitzman, M. (1984) *The Share Economy: Conquering Stagflation*, Cambridge, Mass: Harvard University Press.

Weitzman, M. L. (1985a) 'Profit sharing as macro-economic policy', *American Economic Review*, LXXV, May, pp. 41–5.

Weitzman, M. L. (1985b) 'The simple macro-economic policy', *American Economic Review*, LXXV, Dec, pp. 937–53.

Wellens, J. (1974) 'Employee participation through shareholding', *Industrial and Commercial Training*, VI, 10, Oct, pp. 459–63.

Wellens, J. (1977) 'Employee funds', *Industrial and Commercial Training*, IX, 5, May, pp. 183–6.

Westway, J. E. and Jacobs, E. R. (1958) 'The nature of profit sharing schemes', *Personnel Practice Bulletin*, 14 Dec.

Whyte, W. F. (1978) 'Ownership control and participation', paper presented to the International Sociology Association, Uppsala, Sweden, quoted in Sockell, D. (1985) 'Attitudes, behavior and employee ownership: some preliminary data', *Industrial Relations*, 24, 1, pp. 130–8.

Whyte, W. F., Hammer, T. H., Meek, C. B., Nelson, R. and Stern, R. N. (1983) *Worker Participation and Ownership*, Cornell: Industrial and Labor Relations Press.

White, P. J. (1980) 'Share ownership schemes for employees: proposals and projects', *Managerial and Decision Economics*, 3.

Wigham, E. L. (1973) *The Power to Manage*, London: Macmillan.

Williams, A. (1913) *Co-Partnership and Profit Sharing*, London: Williams and Norgate.

Wilpert, B. and Sorge, A. (eds) (1984) *International Yearbook of Organizational Democracy*, II, Chichester: Wiley.

Wilson, D. (1977–8) 'Profit sharing and employee shareholding in ICI', *Industrial Participation*, DLXIII, Winter, pp. 10–17.

Wilson, D. and Davies, T. J. (1977–8), 'Profit sharing case histories', *Industrial Participation*, DLXIII, Winter, pp. 10–24.

Woodworth, W. (1981a) 'Forms of employee ownership and workers' control', *Sociology of Work and Occupations*, 8, 2, May, pp. 195–200.

Woodworth, W. (1981b) 'Towards a labor owned economy in the United States', *Labor and Society*, 6, 1, Jan/March, pp. 41–56.

Index